FINALLY a locally produced

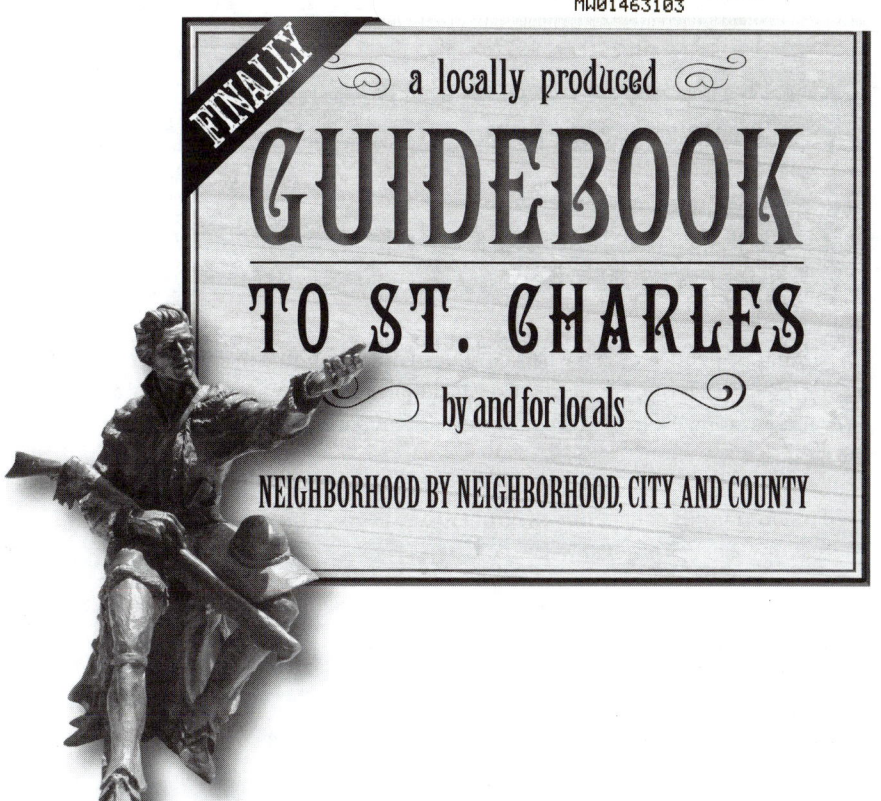

GUIDEBOOK
TO ST. CHARLES
by and for locals

NEIGHBORHOOD BY NEIGHBORHOOD, CITY AND COUNTY

JUSTINE RIGGS AND VICKI BERGER ERWIN

Enjoy St. Charles!
Justine Riggs
Vicki Berger Erwin

Copyright © 2015, Reedy Press
All rights reserved.

Reedy Press
PO Box 5131
St. Louis, MO 63139, USA

No part of this publication may be reproduced or transmitted in any form or by any means, electronic or mechanical, including photocopy, recording, or any information storage and retrieval system, without permission in writing from the publisher.

Permissions may be sought directly from Reedy Press at the above mailing address or via our website at www.reedypress.com.

Library of Congress Control Number: 2014958914

ISBN: 9781935806936

Please visit our website at www.reedypress.com.

Design by Barbara Northcott

Printed in the United States of America
15 16 17 18 19   5 4 3 2 1

Disclaimer: Locations have been selected by the authors and are not inclusive of all that St. Charles has to offer. At press time, information was correct to our knowledge.

CONTENTS

Acknowledgments v

Historic Main Street 1

Frenchtown 57

St. Charles 65

St. Peters 97

Cottleville 117

O'Fallon 125

Lake St. Louis 149

Wentzville 157

Augusta/Defiance/New Melle 175

Portage des Sioux 199

Helpful Websites 205

Photo Credits 207

Index 209

🐾 Pet friendly

kids Kid friendly

💍 Wedding resource

ACKNOWLEDGMENTS

As a 20-year citizen of St. Charles County (the majority of those as a St. Charles City resident), I am so proud to live within a community that has so much to offer visitors and locals alike. I never tire of exploring the area and finding new and exciting things to do.

I am grateful to Josh Stevens for the opportunity to work with Reedy Press again. Thank you for believing in me. Many thanks to Barbara Northcott, who tirelessly endured countless edits with continuous patience.

To my co-author, Vicki Erwin, I am thankful for the experience you brought to this project, but most of all for our newfound friendship. What an absolute pleasure it was co-creating with you.

This project was a true collaboration. Thank you to all the residents, business owners, and citizens within the county who took time to speak with us and to share your photos. It brought me much joy to see how many of you also truly love where you live and work.

Finally, much love to my family and friends, who continue to support me in my writing endeavors. I am especially blessed for my husband, Kevin, and daughter, Kalei. It means the world to me that you both always encourage me to follow my dream and passion for writing. Lastly, I cannot forget to thank my furry family members who keep me company at all hours of the night when the writing process gets a little crazy.

-Justine Riggs

I worked in St. Charles, specifically on Main Street, for a number of years and constantly encouraged people to visit because I knew they had no idea how much there was to see and do. How great is it to be part of a book that will spread the word about the virtues of St. Charles, both the city and county, even more widely!

So, thank you, Reedy Press and Josh Stevens, for including me in this project.

Mega-thanks to co-author Justine Riggs for inviting me to share this experience. You are easy and fun to work with, but best of all a true professional. I loved every minute of it (especially coffee and snacks).

Thank you to all the business owners who took time from their busy schedules to talk to me and/or share photos and information. I hope you enjoy the book and will share it with your customers and friends to let them know, too, how great the city and county are.

An especially warm thanks to Carol Felzien and Pam Schulz from the Greater St. Charles Convention and Visitors Bureau. I truly don't know if we would have been able to have a book without all your help and input.

And thanks and love always to my family, especially my husband, Jim who now knows what it is like to write books on deadline.

Thank you to Barbara Northcott for making the book better!

Photo credits: Many of the photos used in this book were provided by individuals and organizations. Credit goes to the Greater St. Charles Convention & Visitors Bureau, which generously shared photos as well as Remington's, Holly Haddox, Michael Henry, and for original artwork Linda Wilmes (St Charles Mural) and Serena Boschert (Main Street Doors). Thank you.

-Vicki Berger Erwin

ST. CHARLES NEIGHBORHOODS – HISTORIC MAIN STREET

HISTORIC MAIN STREET

Main Street is where it all begins—the history, the shopping, the dining, the fun. As one of the largest historic shopping districts in Missouri, Main Street St. Charles has it all.

Louis Blanchette became the first permanent white settler in 1769 when he and wife, Angelique, built a dwelling at what is now 906 S. Main Street. He chose the location because of its proximity to the river, making travel easy. Blanchette called it "Les Petite Côtes"—the small hills—because of the hills rising from the river. Like Blanchette, most early settlers to the area were French, yet they lived under the Spanish flag. Soon, the community was called San Carlos de la Rio Misuri—St. Charles on the Missouri River. In 1800, in a secret deal, France took control of the area, placing it under the French flag only long enough to sell it to the United States in 1803.

In 1804, soon after the Louisiana Purchase, Lewis and Clark set out on their voyage of westward discovery from St. Charles. In the years between Blanchette's settlement and Lewis and Clark's journey, the town grew to approximately 400 residents with 100 buildings. Most of the residents were still French, an influence that can be seen in the style of architecture of the buildings standing today.

As the country grew, St. Charles became a popular location to embark upon western journeys once those lands were opened for settlement. Businesses that catered to these travelers became an important part of the city. Settlers from Kentucky, Tennessee, the Carolinas, and Virginia also settled in the area, following the lead of explorer Daniel Boone, who was enticed to the area with a land grant in hopes that he would encourage others to follow him.

In 1820, St. Charles was considered the population center of the state with 1,200 residents. Upon Missouri's admission to the Union as a state in 1821, St. Charles was named the state capital. The city remained the capital until

1826. The buildings that housed the first legislative session of the state have been restored and are open to the public as a Missouri State Historic Site.

New settlers from Germany flocked to St. Charles and the surrounding area in the mid-to-late 1800s. Living conditions in parts of Germany were less than ideal, and a book published in Germany by Gottfried Duden, a German who had traveled to Missouri, touted the countryside as similar to that of the Rhineland and described the area as a land of opportunity. The German influx bolstered the population and grew the economic base of St. Charles.

St. Charles continued to thrive and grow with Main Street as a center until the 1960s, when population began to shift westward. Many of the buildings on Main Street fell into disrepair, including the former state capitol. A group of forward-thinking citizens banded together in an effort to save the capitol, which led to the purchase and renovation of the building by the state of Missouri. That in turn promoted efforts to preserve the surrounding area after South Main Street was named to the National Register of Historic Places in June 1970. The preservation efforts spread to North Main Street and Frenchtown as well. Today St. Charles is a model for restoration and preservation projects.

There are several ways to experience Main Street: as a historical center, as a vacation destination, and as a shopping haven.

SHOPPING

If shopping is your bag, Main Street is your place. Walk along the same street where long ago pioneers shopped. (You cannot escape history in St. Charles!) Keep in mind that about one-third of the shops are closed on Monday and a smaller number on Sunday. If you are interested in visiting a particular merchant on one of those two days of the week, you may want to call first. Hours may also vary depending on the day of the week or season. Parking is available on the street (free), in parking lots along Riverside Drive (free), and in the Municipal Parking Garage (fee). Pay attention to the hour limits posted in some areas; you will be ticketed! Unfortunately, because so many of the buildings on Main Street are historic, there is limited handicapped accessibility.

Please be sure to note whether the business you are looking for is on NORTH Main or SOUTH Main as numbers may repeat.

ALL THAT GLITTERZ
A shop featuring fine jewelry as well as silver and fashion jewelry.

(636) 724-0400
523 S Main St.

ANTIQUES & OAK
Antiques & Oak carries everything from antique tables to the dinnerware you'll set them with. They buy, sell, and appraise.

(636) 946-1898
319 N Main St.
www.antiquesnoak.com

APRIL'S ON MAIN
Opened in June 2014, April's on Main offers a lovely selection of home and personal accessories. April worked for many years at the Flower Petaler and now brings her wealth of experience to her own shop. Her displays are sure to send you away with all kinds of new decorating ideas. April is also a cat lover and has personally rescued and homed over 800 cats! She continues to work on this "pet" project in her new location.

(636) 395-7605
222 N Main St.
aprilsonmain@gmail.com
www.aprilsonmain.com

BAUBLES, BITES & BOOTS
"Something neat, something sweet, something to put upon your feet" is a description of what you will find at BB&B. They carry accessories, gifts, spices and goodies, jewelry, and footwear

(especially boots). Check out their assortment of accessories to dress up your boots!

(636) 757-3712
107 N Main St.

THE BRIDGE FAIR TRADE MARKET

The Bridge is run by an ecumenical ministry that works to bring justice and hope to the world both locally and globally. It is an extension of the Bridge Coffee House in New Town. With a purchase of unique fair market goods created by artisans, craftsmen, and farmers in developing countries (and locally), the buyer helps combat hunger and homelessness, combat human trafficking, and provide clean water, educational supplies and schools, and job training. There are also volunteer opportunities available to become further involved in this mission.

(636) 493-9733
418 S Main St.
www.thebridge-online.org

CANINE COOKIES N CREAM DOG BAKERY

Feel bad leaving your dog at home while you have fun in St. Charles? Then bring him along to pick out a treat, toy, or outfit. The bakery treats look good enough for humans to eat!

(636) 443-2266
822 S Main St.
mk9lvr@gmail.com
www.caninecookiesncream.com

CASSANDRA ERIN STUDIO

For a unique, one-of-a-kind jewelry piece, the Cassandra Erin Studio is a sure bet. Cassie crafts pendants, bracelets, rings, key chains, and more using the customer's own handwriting and words, perhaps a piece of art by a beloved child, or even handprints or footprints. Pieces from this collection are called "From the Heart" and are very lovely. Other lines are also offered as well as the work of fellow artists.

(636) 573-0133
112 S Main St.
cassie@cassandraerin.com
www.cassandraerin.com

CENTURIES PAST ANTIQUES

Located at the rear of My Handyworks, Centuries Past sells antiques, vintage collectibles, and memorabilia.

(636) 946-1919
104 S Main St. Rear

COBBLESTONE COTTAGE

Cobblestone Cottage is the go-to shop for American Country and Colonial reproduction furniture and accessories. The large showroom features furniture, linens, artwork, lighting, and more.

(636) 949-0721
803 S Main St.
cwoodcobblestone@yahoo.com
www.cobblestonesaintcharles.com

COUNTRY HOUSE
Features American country-style home furnishings and gifts.

(636) 926-2789
915 S Main St.

DESIGNER LIKE
Shop here for designer-inspired handbags, trendy jewelry, accessories, and Juelle pet accessories.

(636) 916-3290
415 S Main St.
juellepetproducts@yahoo.com
www.designerlikeonmain.com

DI OLIVAS
Di Olivas offers a variety of balsamic vinegars, olive oil, and other gourmet food products. The staff is eager to help you use their products to bring out their best qualities. The mix includes 15 flavors of balsamic vinegars, two dozen flavors of pasta, the recently added gourmet coffee bean collection, and of course the olive oils. Di Olivas offers their customers the best and freshest 100% extra virgin olive oils (EVOO) from seven countries. EVOO is revered for its health benefits but also has unique flavors based on its origins. One of the advantages of shopping for your product at this shop is being able to sample before buying to make sure you are getting exactly what you desire. Customers are also invited to submit successful recipes they have created using products purchased at the shop to the Di Olivas website to share with others.

(636) 724-8282
617 S Main St.
www.diolivas.com

ELEMENTS HERBAL APOTHECARY
The folks at Elements seek to assist customers in applying herbs throughout their entire lives. There are herbs to sustain the body, herbs used to create aromatherapy products, cooking herbs, and a line of natural bath and body products available at this new Main Street destination.

(314) 780-4219
700 S Main St.
www.elementsapothecary.com

THE ENCHANTED ATTIC
Don't miss this mystical shop that sells unique jewelry, music, tarot cards, incense, crystals, metaphysical books and more.

(636) 949-9502
304 S Main St.

ENCHANTMENTS
This woman's boutique features clothing, shoes, and accessories.

(636) 724-3335
809 S Main St.

THE ENGLISH SHOP
Entering the English Shop is like visiting an English village shop in the middle of Missouri. Since 1984, the staff has been bringing the finest in English food and gifts to homesick Englishmen or to those who

are simply hungry for an English lifestyle. Today the shop features the largest British food selection in the Midwest. Some of the products include candy (Cadbury's!), biscuits, jams, teas, mugs, teapots, cookbooks, and much, much more. The building was a customs house when the area was under Spanish rule. All travelers were required to stop for inspection and to obtain a permit to travel west. The top floor was used to accommodate overnight travelers and the backyard was a stable for horses and livestock.

(636) 946-2245
703 S Main St.
www.theenglishshoponline.com

EUROPEAN ACCENT

European Accent carries a variety of ladies clothing and accessories, home décor, and custom floral décor.

Some of the lines include Mariana jewelry (one of the largest dealers in the Midwest), Vera Bradley, Baggallini (including seasonal colors), Betsey Johnson, Papillon, Samuel Dong, Vocal, Firefly jewelry, and more.

(636) 724-7677
426 S Main St.
www.europeanaccent.net

FANCY FEET SHOE BOUTIQUE

The shoe boutique features unique shoe lines for women and girls.

(636) 724-8400
508 S Main St.
www.fancyfeetshoeboutique.com

FIGUERO'S

Keep going from room to room to room in Figuero's to make sure you see everything it carries in this gourmet food and espresso shop. Choose from more than 100 different fresh-roasted gourmet coffees and bag and loose teas, as well as accessories to serve hot beverages—lovely teapots, mugs, and more. The store also offers baking mixes, dips, soups, spices, and more. But the pièce de résistance is the over 2,000 hot sauces to choose from, the largest selection of hot sauces west of the Mississippi. If shopping finally has you worn out, relax in the espresso bar overlooking the Missouri River and enjoy a selection of hot or cold beverages.

(636) 947-9847
524 S Main St.

FINISHING TOUCHES BY CHARLOTTE

Whether it is your home, your garden, or yourself that needs a finishing touch, Charlotte's will have it. The shop is six rooms, each a different flavor, of unique merchandise that will make shopping a pleasure.

(636) 947-6330
825 S Main St.
www.finishingtouchesbycharlotte.com

FIRST CAPITOL TRADING

First Capitol Trading has been in business since 1967, bringing high-quality collectibles, jewelry, accessories, and décor to Main Street. They carry Jim Shore, Precious Moments, Lladro, Pandora, and Christopher Radko, to name a few. The shop features holiday-themed ornaments and collectibles as well as the perfect gift for special occasions. It is a treat just to browse the shop.

Hours vary seasonally.
(636) 946-2883
207 S Main St.
www.firstcapitoltrading.com

THE FLOWER PETALER/ HOLIDAY HOUSE

Enter the world of the Flower Petaler and journey through 17 rooms of enticing home décor, holiday decorations, silk florals, accessories, Heritage Lace, and more—over 100,000 items. A customer never knows what delightful surprise is waiting around the next corner. Keep in mind, the Flower Petaler is more than florals! In business for 42 years, the store is one of the longest-running businesses under continuous ownership on Main Street. The friendly and knowledgeable staff will also assist with in-home Christmas decorating, in-home decorating, and wedding silk florals. The Holiday House offers a year-round selection of the best in Christmas decorations including Olde World, Department 56, Christopher Radko, and Fontanini, among others.

(636) 946-3048
620 S Main St.
www.flowerpetaler.net

FOX & HOUND ANTIQUES & DÉCOR

The Fox & Hound location at 319 S. Main Street displays (with great flair) antique and vintage items from 12 different dealers. Fox & Hound recently added a second location at 604 S. Main Street with the slogan "A sly mix of new and old," and that shop has even more great antique and vintage furniture and vintage jewelry, mixed with new décor, jewelry, and gift items. The newest trend in home décor may be displayed on a treasured antique pharmacy cabinet to show each in its best light. Check back often as there are always new items coming in. The original location makes its home in a former stagecoach stop and hangout for legislators when St. Charles was the state capital. The newer location is located behind Joys by Austen Warren Design.

(314) 660-2847
604 S Main St.
danielhobbs1020@yahoo.com
www.fandhantiques.com

FRAMATIONS CUSTOM FRAMING AND ART GALLERY

Framations Art Gallery features exhibitions of work by resident artists as well as thematic exhibits in a variety of media. You may purchase artwork and take classes with resident artists. Custom framing and matting is also offered. Their website is excellent, and if you miss an exhibit, it is available to view online!

(636) 724-8313
218 N Main St.
framations@earthlink.net
www.framations.com

FRAN'S

Fran's is a shopping delight, carrying an array of products including Lampe Berger lamps and fragrances, therapeutic magnetic jewelry, art glass, fashion jewelry, Franz porcelain, soaps, candles, and more.

(636) 940-1919
427 S Main St.

FRIPERIE

The Friperie is a unique gift shop offering a wide array of items, including holiday and monogrammed pieces as well as home and personal accessories. If you aren't quite ready to scrapbook, take a look at the magnetic boards with scrapbook-like magnets to create a photo array in your home or on your refrigerator and then change it at will. Halloween hats will glamorize any beautiful witch! And remember their slogan—"Cute boutique with gifts for everyone on your list . . . including yourself."

(636) 947-7980
610 S Main St.

GENE'S SHOES

Gene bought into the shoe business in 1948, starting with women's shoes in hard-to-find sizes and then adding men's shoes. Once his daughter became a pedorthist, the store added shoe modification for customers with foot conditions. It is a great place to find comfortable yet stylish shoes.

(636) 946-1652
126 N Main St.
www.genesshoes.com

GIFT NOOK

Shoppers will find a little bit of everything in this eclectic shop including German nutcrackers, miniatures, and dollhouse furniture.

(636) 946-7666
413 S Main St.

GINSEY ROSE
Ginsey Rose is an eclectic boutique featuring unique, vintage items, button jewelry, necklaces and bracelets made of old clock and watch parts, initial earrings, and many other interesting pieces of clothing and accessories. Some of the items, such as the button jewelry and initial earrings, are created from vintage elements by the shop owner.

(636) 219-4029
902 S Main St.

GRANDMA'S COOKIES
As Grandma says, "A balanced diet is a cookie in each hand." This cozy shop features home-baked cookies that are a hit with cookie lovers from all over the country—check out the map with pins indicating where visitors have come from. During festivals and special events, the shop expands to a tent alongside their building to accommodate the crowds wanting to buy their product. Choose from chocolate chip, snickerdoodle, peanut butter, peanut butter chocolate chip, and more, including special seasonal flavors. All cookies are handmade daily from the finest ingredients. If you happen by at the right moment, the cookies will still be warm from the oven!

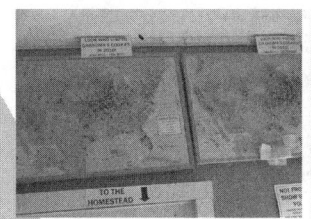

(636) 947-0088
401 S Main St. (shares a building with the Homestead)
info@grandmascookiesonmain.com
www.grandmascookiesonmain.com

HARDWARE OF THE PAST
If your antique chest is missing a pull or you have scratches on an accent table, Hardware of the Past, with its extensive collection of antique reproduction hardware and refinishing aids, can help. In addition, the store and online shop also carry replacement parts and pieces for antique furniture, cane and wicker repair supplies, and more.

(636) 724-3771
405 N Main St.
hopinfo@hardwareofthepast.com
www.hardwareofthepast.com

HIDE & CHIC BY DOUBLE K LEATHER
(636) 493-1833
205 N Main St.
www.doublekleather.com

HOBBIT'S HOLE ANTIQUES
Wander through 12 rooms of fine to whimsical antiques and collectibles.

(636) 947-6227
1019 S Main St.

THE HOMESTEAD

"Where Country and Traditional Home Décor Meet."

(636) 946-2700
401 S Main St.
www.thehomesteadinstcharles.com

J. NOTO BAKERY FINE ITALIAN CONFECTIONS

J. Noto is a family owned and operated business that specializes in delectable treats. They are well known for their authentic Italian pastries, especially the cannoli and tiramisu, and they also carry a variety of chocolates, desserts, cookies, and cakes.

(636) 949-0800
336 S Main St.
jaspernoto@gmail.com
www.jnoto.com

JAKE'S ON MAIN

Jake's on Main is an independently owned shop that sells top-quality Life is good® merchandise designed for a casual lifestyle.

Hours are adjusted seasonally.

(636) 724-9992
136 S Main St.
www.jakesonmainstcharles.com

JANSENS JEWELRY, CLOCKS & GIFTS

One of the gifts on everyone's wish list is time, and you can find precisely this at Jansens. Clocks in all their glory line the shelves and walls of this timely store. The grandfather clocks are sure to become family heirlooms. But there are also unique rhythm clocks, cuckoo clocks, mantel clocks, and wall clocks. Jansens has recently added fine jewelry including diamonds, estate, and vintage jewelry to their stock mix. And if you are looking for a way to cheer your favorite team, the store has a line of team memorabilia for your favorite. (Go Cards!) Jansens also services and repairs jewelry and timepieces. Don't waste any more time—visit today.

(636) 949-0033
608 S Main St.
www.jansensclocks.com

JOHN DENGLER, TOBACCONIST

Enter this historic building and be surrounded with the rich aroma of tobacco. The building dates to 1805 and was a popular eating and drinking establishment for legislators during the days that St. Charles served as the state capital. Although the tobacco shop doesn't date back quite that far, it has been in business under the same family's ownership since 1917. During those almost 100 years, the proprietors and staff have created many popular tobacco blends that are still available at John Dengler's today. They offer the finest in imported pipes, tobaccos, cigars, and smokers' accessories. Hand-blended custom smoking mixtures are also available.

(636) 946-6899
700 S Main St.
Jdengler1917@yahoo.com
www.johndenglertobacconist.com

JOYS BY AUSTIN WARREN DESIGN
Visit this shop for a selection of home décor, estate items, gifts, and floral.

(636) 724-2124
600 S Main St.

KERNEL DAVE'S GOURMET POPCORN
Kernel Dave's is located above the Little Hills Wine Shop and offers a variety of gourmet and flavored popcorn. Gift baskets, tins, and snacks are also available.

(636) 946-9165
710 S Main St.
www.kerneldaves.com

LA GALLERIE
This gallery displays and sells affordable oil paintings and prints including landscapes, seascapes, and street scenes.

(636) 949-9644
812 S Main St.

LA ROSERIE
La Roserie provides a unique shopping experience featuring eclectic home décor with many items created by local artisans.

(314) 265-4942
700 S Main St.
laroserie@yahoo.com
www.laroserie.com

LADY BUGS
Lady Bugs carries a wide array of gift items for home and garden including Willow Tree, Jim Shore, greeting cards, plush, and a variety of flags. Honoring the name, there is a delightful display of ladybug-themed items for your gift shopping.

(636) 724-2747
719 S Main St.
ladybugsonmain@gmail.com

LAURA'S LA PETITE
Note the architecture of the building housing Laura's La Petite. If it reminds you of a blacksmith shop, that's because it served as one in the 1890s. The Schemmer brothers ran the shop and lived in twin houses nearby. The cornices and arches show the skill of the German artisans who laid the brick. The arched window was formerly a doorway that wagons passed through to the rear of the building to be repaired. Today Laura's offers a carefully curated collection of new and vintage treasures including Missouri creations by Laura and her friends.

(636) 724-4207
709 S Main St.

LILLIAN'S
Lillian's is a franchise shop with locations around the country, including one in St. Charles. The store is open limited hours each month and offers affordable yet stylish fashions and accessories.

(636) 255-0295
124 S Main St.
stcharles@lilliansshoppe.com
www.lilliansshoppe.com/stcharles

LITTLE HILLS COTTAGE
Offers jewelry at discount prices with new products arriving constantly.

Open weekends only
(636) 925-0622
335 S Main St.
www.littlehillscottage.net

LITTLE HILLS WINE SHOP
Located a few blocks from the companion restaurant, this shop is the official outlet for Little Hills Wines. Little Hills has produced award-winning wines for more than 20 years and has grown to be one of the largest wineries in Missouri. The store also offers wine accessories and gifts for wine lovers.

(636) 946-6637
710 S Main St.
www.littlehillsshops.com

MAIN STREET BOOKS
Main Street Books is a gem of a bookstore with two floors of books to fit every interest and age. The store carries a wide selection of books about the local area as well as a great selection of children's books. MSB works closely with local schools and libraries to bring authors to St. Charles and to build interest in books and reading. There is a frequent buyer program and monthly book clubs.

(636) 949-0105
307 S Main St.
mainstreetbooksstcharles@gmail.com
www.mainstreetbooks.net

kids

MAIN STREET MARKETPLACE
The charming former residence built in the German style in the 1850s is the perfect setting for this shop offering a variety of specialty foods including spices, seasonings, sauces, coffees, teas, jams, and jellies, as well as gifts and home décor and accessories. Main Street Marketplace has its own brand of specialty foods for your family's appetites. Offerings of samples throughout the store only add to the flavor of a visit to MSM.

(636) 940-8626
708 S Main St.
skipulliam@aol.com
www.mainstreetmarketplace.com

MAIN STREET ROOT BEER AND SODA
Located above Di Olivas is Main Street Root Beer and Soda, offering 200 different glass-bottled sodas and root beers, floats, jerky, and salty treats.

(636) 724-8282
617 S Main St.

MARIE ANGELIQUE BRA AND LINGERIE
Marie Angelique offers bras and lingerie that provide comfort, quality, and design for all body types. The staff is available

for consultation and is committed to making sure that each person achieves the right fit. The store carries everything for your bra and lingerie needs from everyday underwear to bridal intimates for your wedding day. The shop also carries mastectomy products. Marie Angelique is available for private events such as bridal showers.

(636) 949-2348
220 N Main St.
info@marieangelique.com
www.marieangelique.com

MASTER'S PIECES FINE JEWELRY & GIFTS
View the work of more than 70 artists on sale at Master's Pieces. Owner and jewelry designer Babs Hall specializes in wedding and engagement rings but will work with customers on custom designs for other pieces. Repairs are also available.

(636) 925-1333
816 S Main St.
babettejbh@hotmail.com
www.masterspiecesonmain.com

MEMORIES IN THE ATTIC
Step back into childhood upon entering Memories in the Attic. The shop carries quilts, Lee Middleton and Ashton Drake dolls, dollhouse furniture, and Bearington Bears.

(636) 946-3833
328 S Main St.

MISSOURI ARTISTS ON MAIN
At this artists' co-op, view (and purchase) the work of more than 20 award-winning Missouri artists in a variety of media including paintings, photography, ceramics, fiber arts, and more. The gallery and studio also offers classes taught by the artists.

(636) 724-1260
321 S Main St.
jmcmullenart@aol.com
www.maomgallery.com

MISSOURI MERCANTILE
Missouri Mercantile features a selection of Missouri-made products from the finest artists, artisans, and growers, including a wide selection of wines, gift baskets, food items, and books.

(314) 323-2051
904 S Main St.
info@missourimercantile.com
www.missourimercantile.com

MOSS BOUTIQUE

Owned by a former fashion designer, this shop has the know-how to succeed in the fashion world while helping you succeed in the world with your fashion choices. Moss is a unique boutique offering the latest styles and accessories from many designer labels including the owner's. It is also the go-to store on Main Street for the popular Alex and Ani line of bracelets and jewelry.

(636) 410-0625
424 S Main St.
info@shoptiques.com
www.mossboutique.com

MY HANDYWORKS

"Where your hands make art." My Handyworks is an interactive art studio that started out with only a couple of designs made from a handprint. Today there are many more designs you can use as well as making the ever popular wax hands. The studio offers classes and camps, and will host your party. Don't forget to say hi to Woody the parakeet.

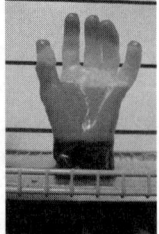

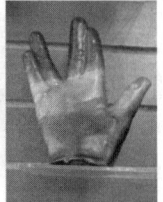

(636) 724-7337
104 S Main St.
myhandyworks@hotmail.com
www.myhandyworks.com

Kids

NATIVE TRADITIONS GALLERY

Native Traditions Gallery specializes in Native American art and jewelry. They have a wide selection of turquoise jewelry on display and for sale. There are interesting sculptures and unique tables hewn from redwood tree trunks, polished but naturally shaped. Chico the Bird will not let you escape without a few words and/or a little attention.

(636) 947-0170
310 S Main St.

NIC NAC STOP

Visit the Nic Nac Stop for a unique selection of handcrafted items for all occasions.

(636) 724-7299
525 S Main St.
www.nic-nac-stop.com

OLDE TOWN SPICE SHOPPE

Walking into Olde Town Spice Shoppe is a sensory delight! Their slogan is "Making life delicious since 1983," and their wide selection of spices, herbs, seasonings, teas, sauces, marinades, and more help make this come true. This family-run business truly believes that family, friends, and food create great memories, and it is their goal to help each customer do that by offering advice on how to cook and use their products, finding recipes, and providing lovely utensils and gifts to use as service items. The store is located in the former home of the brothers Millington, two of St. Charles's first physicians. These men, in their day, made St. Charles the center of the castor oil industry.

(636) 916-3600
334 S Main St.
spice@oldtownspices.com
www.oldtownspices.com

OOH LA LA

Ooh La La is a boutique carrying unique ladies' fashions as well as accessories, jewelry, shoes, and socks.

(636) 940-2020
340 S Main St.

OOH LA LA CHILDREN'S BOUTIQUE

A companion boutique for Ooh La La just for children! The shop carries adorable clothing from newborn sizes up to boys and girls. Choose also from their baby gifts, toys, and accessories.

(636) 940-0202
519 S Main St.

POOR MAN'S ART GALLERY

This gallery offers a large selection of art at affordable prices.

(636) 949-5237
506 S Main St.

POPPY'S AMISH CUPBOARD

Visit Poppy's for a selection of genuine Amish foods and custom-made, one-of-a-kind furniture and gift items.

(314) 732-3289
720 S Main St.

PROVENANCE SOAPWORKS

The scent alone makes it worthwhile to step inside Provenance Soapworks! As they advertise, "sniffs are free." The shop sells locally produced soaps and beauty products, made in small batches to assure quality. The ingredients are natural and only paraben-free preservatives are used. (Preservatives are necessary to keep the products from deteriorating too rapidly.) A favorite product is the sugar scrub (in various "flavors") that exfoliates, moisturizes, and cleanses all at once. Visit the scent bar where customers may blend their own fragrances. And be on the lookout for new products to come!

(636) 577-1972
311 S Main St.

THE QUILTED COTTAGE

A new Main Street addition, the Quilted Cottage is a full-service quilt shop with fabric, patterns, books, and wool appliqué kits.

(636) 757-3730
723 S Main St.
www.thequiltedcottageonmain.com

REMINGTON'S

Remington's is a balloon specialist offering balloon décor for any special occasion. Delivery available in Missouri and Illinois.

(636) 946-7663
302 N Main St.
scberthold@sbcglobal.net
www.remingtonsballoons.com

RIVERSIDE SWEETS

Need a sweet snack? Riverside Sweets is the place to go for handmade candies and ice cream treats galore. Candies are available by the pound or bagged to go, and include fudge, brittles, caramel, toffees, chocolates, and more. While you are refilling the energy meter, shop their selection of seasonal décor. Always a treat!

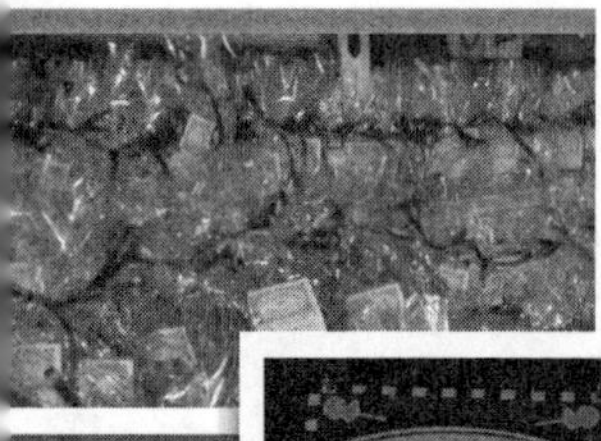

(636) 724-4131
416 S Main St.

SCENTCHIPS ST. CHARLES

Scentchips are the original fragrance melt, offering handmade-in-America home fragrance melts since 1979. There are 40 fragrances available, but customers are welcome to create their own signature scent. An accessory line complements the fragrances available. ATM on premises.

(636) 916-5600
612 S Main St.
www.stcharles.scentchips.com

SCHNARR JEWELERS/ DREAMCATCHER

Schnarr's carries authentic Native American jewelry from many tribes, purchased directly from the reservation. They also carry estate jewelry, quilts, collectibles, vintage jewelry, flutes, dreamcatchers, and much more.

(636) 255-8885
724 S Main St.
www.schnarrjewelers.com

SIOSTRA

Siostra is the home of the second-largest Polish pottery store in Missouri. The name means "sister" in Polish and honors the owner's two sisters and five sisters-in-law. The Polish pottery in the shop is both beautiful and functional. It is oven-, microwave-, and dishwasher-safe, and it comes in compatible designs that mix and match to perfection. The store also offers Polish cooking classes taught by professional chefs once a month at a reasonable charge. Siostra carries other imported gifts including Lithuanian candle houses and Italian rooster pitchers. The entire mix is displayed in a delightful and charming setting along Stone Row.

(636) 925-1480
330 S Main St.
info@potterystcharlesmo.com
www.potterystcharlesmo.com

STITCHES, ETC

Stitches, Etc is a fun sewing shop that specializes in cross-stitch and also carries embroidery designs. The staff is eager to help stitchers with their patterns, fabric, fibers, and notions. The shop carries a variety of kits for holiday ornaments. This is a great place to find a gift for your favorite stitcher!

(636) 946-8016
341 S Main St.
stitchesetc@att.net
www.stitches-etc.com

STRING ALONG WITH ME

Located on the lower level of the historic Newbill-McElhiney House, owner Janice hopes to bring out the best in each customer by helping create her own style that complements her body, coloring, and personality. Customers are invited to bring a piece of clothing and Janice will help choose exactly the right jewelry and accessories. If that perfect item(s) is not available in store, Janice will design or find it. String Along With Me carries Brighton accessories as well as an array of unique accessories from other lines.

(636) 947-7740
625 S Main St.

STUDIO GALLO BLU

Studio Gallo Blu is a family-owned art business that has hosted more than 1,000 "sip and paint" classes, parties, and events, both private and public. Please check their calendar of classes or schedule your private "sip and paint" event.

Open by appointment or registration only
(636) 724-5399
205 S Main St.
kate@studiogalloblu.com
www.studiogalloblu.com

THISTLE AND CLOVER

Thistle and Clover specializes in merchandise with a Scottish, Irish, and Welsh flair. Choose from a wide variety of jewelry, glassware, collectibles, and gift items. Need a kilt? This is the place to go. They also have a wide selection of heraldry items available.

(636) 946-2449
407 S Main St.
www.thistleandclover.com

THRO'S CLOTHING COMPANY AND MICHELLE'S

Thro's has been selling men's clothing to residents and visitors to St. Charles's Main Street since 1898! This family-owned business is committed to customer service and quality, making sure that the customer receives the best fit and style. Tuxedo rental is available. Thro's is also the place to shop for your Boy Scout needs. Michelle's offers the same quality selection and service for women, carrying everything from casual wear to evening and mother-of-the-bride gowns.

(636) 724-0132
229 N Main St
www.throsandmichelles.com

TIFFANY GARDEN/GLASS WORKBENCH

The Glass Workbench and Tiffany Garden gift shop are family owned businesses located in a building dating to 1815 and built with 24-inch-thick walls of Burlington limestone. It is part of the set of buildings known in St. Charles as "Stone Row." Tiffany Garden offers art glass gifts for home and garden while the Glass Workbench is a full-service stained glass shop. The Glass Workbench offers stained glass in 500 different colors and textures, fusing supplies, custom-made items and, best of all, classes to learn the art and craft. The company also distributes design books and the mosaic forms for the stained glass stepping stone technique developed by Julie Bishop Day, daughter of the founders.

Open Monday, Tuesday, Thursday, 10 a.m.–5 p.m.; Wednesday, Friday, Saturday, 10 a.m.–8 p.m.; Sunday, noon–5 p.m.
(636) 946-4539
(636) 946-2002
314/318 S Main St.
www.theglassworkbench.com

THE TINTYPERY

For a great souvenir of your visit to Main Street that incorporates a sense of history, have a photo taken in authentic costume (from 1860s to 1920s) at the Tintypery. It's like traveling back in time to have your picture taken. At Christmas (weekends, Thanksgiving through Christmas), Santa has a second headquarters at the studio for photo opportunities in period clothing. You can even bring a furry friend along for an old-time pet portrait.

(636) 925-2155
510 S Main St.
info@tintypery.com
www.tintypery.com

TOODALOO

Toodaloo features hand-painted furniture, vintage items, and a selection of gifts. They also sell Chalk Paint® by Annie Sloan. Check out Toodaloo Too on Second Street in Frenchtown.

(636) 614-4665
201 S Main St.

WALTER'S JEWELRY

Walter's Jewelry is a family-owned business that strives to bring customers the finest in jewelry. Highly skilled jewelers will work with you on custom designs. In-house jewelry repair is available and the staff also offers appraisals.

(636) 724-0604
230 N Main St.
chris@waltersjewelryinc.com
www.waltersjewelryinc.com

RESTAURANTS/DINING

ALICE'S TEA ROOM/THROUGH THE LOOKING GLASS

The tea room serves sandwiches, salads, and desserts, Wednesday through Sunday. Tea parties are available. Through the Looking Glass, a miniature museum, is also housed in the building.

Wednesday through Sunday,
11 a.m.–5 p.m.
(636) 946-0505
329 S Main St.

BELLA VINO WINE BAR & TAPAS

Bella Vino offers high-end wines and a variety of tapas to meet every diner's taste. The atmosphere is friendly, welcoming, and comfortable. The upper level is perfect for a casual, private gathering with drinks and hors d'oeuvres.

Tuesday through Thursday,
4:30 p.m.–10 p.m.
Friday and Saturday,
11 a.m.–midnight
Sunday brunch, 9:30 a.m.–2 p.m.
Sunday dinner, 2 p.m.–9 p.m.
(636) 724-3434

325 S Main St.
www.bellavinowinebarstl.com

BIG A'S ON THE RIVERFRONT

Enjoy one of the best views of the river on Main Street while eating at Big A's. Delight in daily American cuisine and lunch, dinner, and drink specials in a nonsmoking environment. The Riverfront Room is available for parties and special events!

Open Monday through Saturday,
10:30 a.m.–1:30 a.m.
Sunday, 11 a.m.–midnight
(636) 949-9900
308 N Main St.
www.bigasontheriverfront.com

BIKE STOP CAFÉ

Bike Stop Café serves a dual purpose as a bike shop (repair and rental) and an eating establishment. The folks at Bike Stop are committed to social responsibility, healthy eating, and alternative transportation. The menu offers healthy selections for breakfast, lunch, and dinner as well as a coffee menu for that break and pick-me-up. Located slightly off Main Street, on the Katy Trail, both indoor and outdoor dining are available.

Monday through Thursday, 7 a.m.–7 p.m.
Friday and Saturday, 7 a.m.–8 p.m.
Sunday, 7 a.m.–6 p.m.
(636) 724-9900
701 S Riverside Dr.
bikestopcafe@gmail.com
www.bikestopcafes.com

BOBBY'S PLACE
Bobby refers to former St. Louis Blues defenseman Bobby Plager, and Bobby memorabilia decorates the establishment. Food and drink specials seven days a week plus plasma screen TVs to watch sports events, live music, DJs, a jukebox, and games are sure to entertain.

Monday through Saturday, 11 a.m.–1 a.m.
Sunday, 11 a.m.–midnight
(636) 949-2860
143 N Main St.

BOMBSHELL BAR & GRILL
This bar and grill serves lunch, dinner, coffee, appetizers, and drinks, including a daily happy hour. Special events like bingo and trivia as well as music create a lively atmosphere.

Monday through Saturday,
11 a.m.–1:30 a.m.
Sunday, 11 a.m.–midnight
(636) 757-3026
221 N Main St.

BRADDENS RESTAURANT
Enjoy casual fare either inside (non-smoking) or outside on the lovely patio. For an appetizer, try the homemade potato chips. Yummy!

Tuesday through Thursday,
10:30 a.m.–9 p.m.
Friday, 10:30 a.m.–11 p.m.
Saturday, 8:30 a.m.–11 p.m.
Sunday, 8:30 a.m.–7 p.m.
(636) 493-9303
515 S Main St.
www.braddens.vpweb.com

THE COLONIAL TABLE
Dining at the Colonial Table is by reservation only. The experience provides a quality colonial dining experience for 2 to 32 at the lovely Boone's Colonial Inn dining room furnished with 19th-century harvest tables.

(636) 493-1077
326 S Main St.
www.thecolonialtable.com

FRANKIE TOCCO'S PIZZERIA
It's "bon appetito" at Frankie Tocco's. The restaurant's foundation is based on recipes handed down in the Tocco family for over 100 years. Italian food is their forte.

Tuesday through Thursday,
11 a.m.–9 p.m.
Friday, 11 a.m.–10 p.m.
Saturday, noon–10 p.m.
Sunday, noon–8 p.m.
(636) 947-7007
108 S Main St.
www.frankietoccos.com

GARDEN CAFÉ A LA FLEUR

Garden Café offers both inside and patio dining. The lovely patio overlooks the river in a garden setting. The menu is inspired by home-style cooking and the service is friendly and warm.

Monday through Sunday, 11 a.m.–4 p.m.
(636) 493-6023
524 S Main St.
www.gardencafealafleur.com

H.A.M.'S DELI

For a casual lunch of hearty soups and sandwiches, H.A.M.'s Deli is your place. Now serving St. Louis favorite Volpi salami. Join H.A.M.'s for breakfast on Saturday and Sunday.

(636) 578-7889
105 N Main St.
hamsdeli@gmail.com
www.hams-deli.com

HENDRICKS BBQ

Hendricks specializes in down-home Southern foods, including meats smoked daily in-house, fried chicken, meatloaf, and all the fixings, served up with Southern hospitality. You will not go home hungry from Hendricks! Parking is available in the rear. This restaurant is not in the heart of Main Street (it's located in the old waterworks) but it is definitely worth the short walk if you like barbecue.

Monday through Wednesday,
11 a.m.–10 p.m.
Thursday, 11 a.m.–11 p.m.
Friday and Saturday, 11 a.m.–11 p.m.;
bar until 1:30 a.m.
Sunday, 11 a.m.–9 p.m.
(636) 724-8600
1200 S Main St.
www.hendricksbbq.com

LEWIS & CLARK'S RESTAURANT

Lewis & Clark's is a centrally located, landmark restaurant in historic St. Charles. How often does someone say, "I'll meet you at Lewis and Clark's" or "It's near Lewis & Clark's"? They offer an eclectic menu of American cuisine on which everyone is sure to find something they will like. With its ample seating, the restaurant can also host events and parties.

(636) 947-3334
217 S Main St.
www.lewisandclarksrestaurant.com

LITTLE HILLS WINERY AND RESTAURANT

Little Hills features an eclectic menu ranging from soup, salad, and sandwiches to filet mignon, as well as its own locally bottled wines. The patio is available nearly year-round with heating pits located throughout. Live music.

Monday through Thursday,
10:30 a.m.–9:30 p.m.
Friday and Saturday,
10:30 a.m.–11:30 p.m.
Sunday, 10:30 a.m.–8:30 p.m.
(636) 946-9339
501 S Main St.
www.littlehillswinery.com

LITTLE O'S OLD TIME SODA FOUNTAIN

Step back in time when you step into Little O's 1940s soda fountain. From vintage candy to fresh-baked-in-the-store gooey butter cake, you are in for a sweet treat. Enjoy glass bottle sodas and ice cream treats seated at the counter. Feeling like trying something new? Try a gooey butter milkshake that incorporates an entire piece of their famous gooey butter cake. If you pass by on baking day, just one sniff is sure to give you a sugar rush and convince you to come inside and try a piece of gooey butter cake.

(636) 724-0978
125 N Main St.

LLOYD & HARRY'S BAR & GRILL

This intimate bar has a nightclub atmosphere and features daily food and drink specials.

(636) 916-5700
208 N Main St.

LLYWELYN'S PUB

Llywelyn's offers a Celtic dining experience in the heart of historic St. Charles. The building formerly housed a bank and the vault is available for seating. The patio is large and overlooks the river for those lovely days when you want to dine al fresco. The menu includes more than 25 draught and 25 bottled imported, domestic, and craft beers. Celtic-inspired dishes include fried Irish pies, Welsh rarebit, ploughman's melt, shepherd's pie, bangers and mash, and more. Their homemade Welsh potato chips hit the spot. Live music on occasion.

Monday through Saturday,
11 a.m.–1:30 a.m.
Sunday, 11 a.m.–midnight
(636) 724-8520
100 N Main St.
www.llywelynspub.com

MAGPIE CAFÉ

Magpie is open every day for lunch, featuring fresh salads, delicious sandwiches, and best of all, their baked potato soup. Desserts are also a treat. Dinner is served after 5 p.m. and showcases comfort foods, November through March. Seating is available inside, in what used to be the Spanish governor's home in the early days of St. Charles, and outside on a lovely patio. Live music.

Monday through Sunday, 11 a.m.–9 p.m.
Dinner served Monday through Saturday, 5 p.m.–9 p.m.
(636) 947-3883
903 S Main St.
www.magpiesonmain.com

MOTHER-IN-LAW HOUSE RESTAURANT

Delicious home cooking, personal service from the owner, and Victorian décor mark the Mother-in-Law House Restaurant's fine dining experience. Outside dining is also available on a lovely patio overlooking the river. The menu offers comfort food along with a delicious salad bar with homemade dressings. Owner Donna Hafer or one of her longtime servers will bring warm blueberry muffins before the main course and a serving of cooked carrots once your dinner arrives. Save room for the coconut pie—definitely worth forgetting about the diet for a while. Ask Donna or your server for the Mother-in-Law house history. And watch out for ghosts.

Open for lunch, Monday through Saturday, 11 a.m.–2:30 p.m.
Dinner, Tuesday through Saturday, 5:30 p.m.–9:30 p.m.
Also available for private parties
(636) 946-9444
500 S Main St.
www.motherinlawhouse.com

OLD MILLSTREAM INN

The Old Millstream Inn is back after being closed due to a fire several years ago. They have both inside and outside dining and feature an extensive array of beers (over 100 bottled beers) sure to meet everyone's tastes.

Monday, noon–1 a.m.
Tuesday through Saturday, 11 a.m.–1 a.m.
Sunday, noon–midnight
(636) 946-3287
912 S Main St.

PICASSO'S COFFEE HOUSE

Picasso's encourages a local community atmosphere by booking local musicians for entertainment, displaying local artists, and using local roasters and bakers. Each cup of Picasso's coffee is handcrafted, but they serve more than just coffee—bakery goods, sandwiches and salads, and wine, beer, and liqueurs. The comfortable and friendly environment as well as the coffee will bring you back again and again. Much of this book was planned and discussed at Picasso's!

Monday through Wednesday,
6:30 a.m.–9 p.m.
Thursday and Friday, 6:30 a.m.–midnight
Saturday, 7:30 a.m.–midnight
Sunday, 7:30 a.m.–5 p.m.
(636) 925-2911
101 N Main St.
www.picassoscoffeehouse.com

QUINTESSENTIAL DINING & NIGHTLIFE

For an upscale dining and nightlife experience, visit Quintessential. The restaurant and nightclub encompasses three levels including a rooftop patio. Listen to live music every day from 5:30 p.m. to 9 p.m. Thursday through Saturday, a DJ takes the stage at 9 p.m. and the dance floor is open until closing time. Amenities include a smoke-free dance floor (smoking allowed on rooftop), private rooms, four bars, and the rooftop patio with two bars and seven private cabanas. There is also space for your private event.

Monday through Saturday,
11 a.m.–1:15 a.m.
Sunday, 11 a.m.–midnight
(636) 443-2211
149 N Main St.
www.Q-stl.com

R. T. WEILER'S FOOD AND SPIRITS

R. T. Weiler's is located in a historic building that at one time may have changed hands to settle a gambling debt. Longtime residents may remember the building as housing Huning Dry Goods. Today, settle in to a good home-cooked meal ranging from barbecue (or, as it's known at R. T. Weiler's, Bark BQ) to fried chicken, hamburgers to wings, a variety of delicious appetizers, and a wide range of beers. You will find yourself surrounded by pics of customers' dogs—in fact, feel free to bring your own picture of man's or woman's best friend to be displayed in the restaurant. The patio is open to dog guests as well as human.

Open Monday through Thursday,
11 a.m.–11 p.m.
Friday and Saturday, 11 a.m.–1 a.m.
Sunday, 11 a.m.–8 p.m.
(636) 947-1593
201 N Main St.
www.rtweilers.com

TALAYNA'S WORLD CLASS PIZZA

Talayna's offers three styles of pizza: Chicago, New York, and, of course, St. Louis. The menu also includes salads, pastas, sandwiches, and appetizers for dine in or carryout. The restaurant is located at the site of the former Galt Hotel, a place some might say was very unlucky. In 1902, the building was visited by a damaging cyclone; in 1935, railroad cars escaped the Wabash station, crashed into the bridge that was then next door, and then ran right into the hotel. A 40-foot section of the bridge fell onto Main Street, luckily without fatalities. The bridge is no longer there, making Talayna's safe from falling bridgework as well as a great place to eat pizza!

(636) 896-9447
340 N Main St.

TONY'S ON MAIN STREET/ TONY'S ON TOP

Featuring American cuisine, Tony's offers a casual dining experience for lunch and dinner. Enjoy their weekday lunch buffet or a relaxed dinner with the entire family. Catering, both on- and off-site for special events, is available.

Tuesday through Thursday,
11 a.m.–9:30 p.m.
Friday, 11 a.m.–10:30 p.m.
Saturday, noon–10:30 p.m.
Sunday, 4 p.m.–8:30 p.m.
(636) 940-1960
132–136 N Main St.
www.tonysonmain.com

TRAILHEAD BREWING COMPANY

Trailhead is a brewery as well as a casual restaurant. They brew Trailblazer Blond Ale, Trailhead Red Amber Ale, Riverboat Raspberry Beer, Old Courthouse Stout, Missouri Brown Dark Ale, and seasonal selections on-site. The building was originally a woolen mill and during the Civil War operated as a prison for citizens who refused to take the oath of loyalty to the Union.

Sunday through Thursday,
11 a.m.–11 p.m.
Friday and Saturday, 11 a.m.–midnight
(636) 946-2739
921 S Riverside Dr.
www.trailheadbrewing.com

TUNER'S RESTAURANT AND BAR

Tuner's is a bar locals love. They serve lunch Monday through Saturday and serve up live music on the weekends.

Monday through Saturday,
11 a.m.–1:30 a.m.
(636) 724-9212
130 S Main St.

UNCLE JOE'S BAR AND GRILL

Uncle Joe's offers casual dining in a sporty atmosphere. Enjoy games on four high-definition televisions throughout the establishment.

(636) 947-7999
204 N Main St.

UNDERTOW

Enjoy food and drinks in a fun, party atmosphere.

Monday through Saturday,
1 p.m.–1:30 a.m.
Sunday, 1 p.m.–11:30 p.m.
(636) 925-0846
142 N Main St.
www.undertowrestaurant.com

PLACES TO STAY

BOONE'S COLONIAL INN

This boutique inn offers visitors the experience of staying in a quaint 19th-century inn with today's modern conveniences. Depending on how far you want to take your colonial experience, colonial sleeping garments are available as well as lanterns for a late night walk along the riverfront or brick-lined street. The inn is part of Main Street's historic Stone Row, which dates back to 1837. Reservations can be with or without breakfast, which consists of a private breakfast basket with fruit, juice, pastries, and more. The inn is also available for parties and private events.

(636) 493-1077
322 S Main St.
www.boonescolonialinn.com

BOONE'S LICK TRAIL INN/BOONE'S LICK TRAIL COTTAGE

This inn has six rooms and one luxury cottage suite, all with private bath. Lodging includes breakfast. The building housing the inn dates back to 1840, when the Boone's Lick Trail passed by and led travelers to unsettled parts of Missouri and/or to join up with the Oregon or Santa Fe Trails. The cottage is a 1920s-era Arts and Crafts bungalow.

(636) 947-7000
1000 S Main St./1014 S Main St.
innkeeper@booneslick.com
www.booneslick.com

COUNTRY INN AND SUITES
This is a modern facility offering a hot breakfast and indoor pool.

(636) 724-5555
1190 S Main St.
www.countryinns.com/stcharlesmo

MAIN STREET GUEST HOUSE/THE RIVERFRONT GUEST HOUSE/THE OLD TOWN GUEST HOUSE
Three residences on Main Street and Second Street have been luxuriously renovated and made available for rental to visitors to the St. Charles area. The houses may be rented as a group or individually. The Old Town Guest House on Second Street sleeps seven on two levels. The Main Street Guest House sleeps eight on three levels including a master suite on the lower level. This house is located directly on Main Street in the heart of the historic district. The Riverfront Guest House sleeps four on two levels in what was at one time a wheelwright shop that made and repaired wheels for the westward journey. This smaller guesthouse faces the river. All of the guest houses have been renovated to include the charm of old with the amenities and conveniences of the new.

(636) 439-9394

THE MAIN STREET GUEST HOUSE
422 S Main St.

THE RIVERFRONT GUEST HOUSE
422 S Main St., Rear

THE OLD TOWN GUEST HOUSE
320 S Second St.
theguesthouse@centurytel.net
www.theguesthouseco.com

ENTERTAINMENT/THINGS TO DO

FOR THE HISTORY BUFF

If you would like to start with an overview of the history of Main Street, stop by the Greater St. Charles Convention and Visitors Bureau to check out the audio walking tour available at no charge. The tour takes 45 minutes to one hour, depending on how long you linger at each stop. It is also available for preview online at www.historicstcharles.com/things-to-do/video-walking-tour/.

North Main Street has mounted a series of plaques giving the history of many of the buildings and featuring photos from bygone days. These exhibits also present an excellent overview of the area's history and give flavor to a historical journey along Main.

Other locations with historic interest include:

FIRST MISSOURI STATE CAPITOL HISTORIC SITE

St. Charles served as Missouri's first state capital from 1820 to 1826. The location was temporary, as state officials always intended for the capital to be more centrally located.

The state government rented space in two newly constructed, adjoining buildings owned by Charles and Ruluff Peck, who operated a general store on one side, and Chauncy Shepard, who operated a carpentry shop on his side. The second floor was converted into legislative chambers for the house and senate and the governor's office. After the capital moved to Jefferson City, the building returned to its former use.

Through the years, the building housed various businesses, but over time it began to deteriorate and was eventually boarded up. The state acquired the site in 1960 at the behest of a group of interested citizens who worked to save and then restore the capitol to showcase a segment of the state's history. This effort also sparked the renewal and preservation movement on South Main Street. The First State Capitol is now operated as a Missouri State Park.

The buildings have been restored and furnished with 1820s period furniture and are open for tours. The senate and house chambers are on the second floor above the replica store, with the governor's office above a restoration of the Peck family's residence. True to historic detail, the buildings have no electric lighting, only candles, making it a delightful setting for a candlelight concert in December as well as candlelight tours during the holidays.

The legislative chambers (house and senate) sit side by side, separated by only a door. When viewing, keep in mind there were 41 men in the house and 14 senators, most of them rough and tumble, uneducated pioneers. It was not uncommon for physical fights to break out between the legislators when issues became heated. Most of the floor boards are original, although they have been cleaned and restored. Chewing tobacco was common and the rule was to "spit where you sit." Often the results of this rule dripped between the floorboards into the space below.

On the ground floor, visitors may view a store as the Peck brothers might have run it with artifacts from the era. Next door, a typical upper-middle-class home from the era is outfitted with utensils and furniture. Guided and group tours are available.

A gift shop and interpretive center next door to the capitol feature a nice selection of books about Missouri as well as local souvenirs. Exhibits are located on the first and second floor of the interpretive center and include a film about the restoration of the capitol and Main Street.

The capitol hosts special events throughout the year such as Statehood Day, history camp, and a historic children's festival, among others. Tours are $4.50 for adults, $3 for youth aged 6 to 17, and free for children 5 and under.

April through October
Monday through Saturday, 10 a.m.–4 p.m., Sunday, noon–4 p.m.

November and December
Tuesday through Saturday, 10 a.m.–4 p.m., Sunday, noon–4 p.m.

January and February
Tuesday through Saturday, 10 a.m.–4 p.m.

March
Tuesday through Saturday, 10 a.m.–4 p.m., Sunday, noon–4 p.m.

(636) 940-3322
200 S Main St.
www.mostateparks.com/firstcapitol.htm

kids

THE HAVILAND MUSEUM
The Haviland Museum, located in the Newbill-McElhiney House, is the only Haviland museum in the United States. Haviland china dates back to 1842 when David Haviland began buying, then producing, fine china in Limoges, France, and sending it to the United States. The museum contains approximately 1,000

pieces of Haviland china dating from the 1850s, including many unusual pieces.

Tours by appointment only
Admission is $4.50.
Newbill-McElhiney House
(636) 946-9444
625 S Main St.
www.havilandmuseum.com

LEWIS AND CLARK BOAT HOUSE AND NATURE CENTER

On Monday, May 21, 1804, the Lewis and Clark Corps of Discovery left St. Charles, Missouri, to explore the westernmost lands of the Louisiana Purchase and perhaps to find the elusive passage to the Pacific Ocean. After more than two years, to the relief and surprise of the citizens of St. Charles, the party returned on September 21, 1806. The Lewis and Clark Boat House and Nature Center, located on the banks of the Missouri River in a rustic, natural setting, offers an excellent opportunity to grow acquainted with the flora and fauna of the expedition as well as the highlights of the trip itself, including peoples and habitats encountered.

The Boat House is located on the ground floor of the building. Visitors may view replicas of the keelboat, red pirogue, white pirogue, and two dugout canoes used by the Lewis and Clark expedition. The boats were used by the re-enactors of the Discovery Expedition of St. Charles to travel the Lewis and Clark route during the 1804 bicentennial.

The museum itself is located on the second level (elevator available). Displays include a diorama of the expedition's westward journey and a smaller diorama of the trip home, as well as plants and animals encountered, the geology of the lands crossed, a Native American section with artifacts and information about indigenous cultures, mapping equipment and journals, medical care, weather, and the river itself. Other exhibits give a more local view of what St. Charles was like at the time Lewis and Clark visited. Take time to admire the beautiful river views from the large window in the museum room.

There is a classroom with pioneer clothing that children can try on in addition to a collection of articles, photos, and awards collected by the Lewis and Clark Discovery Expedition of St. Charles. The highlight of the classroom visit is a 20-minute film about the expedition full of interesting facts and filmed to give an idea of the open spaces of the new, unsettled land the men encountered.

Outside the building is a Walk of Discovery with plants that would have been growing in the area at the time of Lewis and Clark as well as wildlife, depending upon the time of day and season. This is a prime spot for photos.

The Trading Post, the museum's gift shop, has a great selection of books about Lewis and Clark and Missouri history.

Open Monday through Saturday, 10 a.m.–5 p.m., Sunday, noon–5 p.m. Admission is $5.00 for adults; $2.00 for children under 17; group rates available.
(636) 947-3199
1050 S Riverside Dr.
lewisandclarkmuseum@yahoo.com
www.lewisandclarkcenter.org

OLD BORROMEO CHURCH

The Old Borromeo Church is a reproduction of the original San Carlos Borromeo Church built by Louis Blanchette and dedicated November 7, 1791. The named patron saint for the parish was St. Charles Borromeo, and the church was called San Carlos Borromeo in deference to the Spanish king, Carlos IV. The architecture, which uses upright logs, was the traditional French style and is faithfully reproduced. Once the church was named, the village became known as San Carlos, replacing the earlier Les Petite Côtes. The Old Borromeo Church is located on the spot of the original church.

401 S Main St., Rear

ST. CHARLES COUNTY HISTORICAL SOCIETY

Located in the former Market and Fish House dating to the 1830s, the St. Charles County Historical Society maintains a wealth of information pertaining to the history of St. Charles City and County. The building that now houses the society also served as the St. Charles City Hall and Police Station. The society houses early city and county records pertaining to wills, probate, circuit court, and naturalization as well as more than 15,000 historical photos and a 1,000-volume research library. There are diaries, journals, scrapbooks, personal papers, and information on historic properties available for genealogical and historic research. In addition to the extensive research materials, there is also a small museum with rotating exhibits. The society sponsors events throughout the year to promote St. Charles history as well as classes on genealogy.

Monday, Wednesday, and Friday, 10 a.m.–3 p.m.
Second and fourth Saturdays, 10 a.m.–3 p.m.
Old Market House
(636) 946-9828
101 S Main St.
www.scchs.org

ADDITIONAL POINTS OF INTEREST

THE FOUNDRY ART CENTRE

The Foundry Art Centre anchors the north end of Main Street and is a wonderful example of preservation and repurposing. The building, once owned by American Car and Foundry, was a train car factory. Rather than demolishing the structure when it was no longer needed for manufacturing, the St. Charles community turned it into an art center. The building includes galleries, space for events and performances, and working artists' studios.

The main level opens into the Grand Hall, a large open space lined on either side by gallery space. The Grand Hall provides a venue for performances that have included musician Erin Bode and the St. Louis Wind Symphony as well as Shakespeare and dance performances, to name a few. Every Thursday, visitors can lunch in the Grand Hall from 11:30 a.m. to 1:30 p.m., with catering provided by Spiro's, for an all-inclusive price. The hall is also available for rental for special events.

There are three galleries on the first floor. Gallery I hosts national touring exhibitions across all media. The Ameristar Gallery introduces emerging artists to new audiences. The Baue Family Children's Gallery is a delight, featuring children's artwork from schools across the region. In this gallery, there is also a cozy book corner featuring a selection of illustrated children's books to share with young (and young at heart) visitors.

On the mezzanine level, individual artists' studios are open to viewing. The artists, creating in a variety of media, are often in residence and welcome visitors.

The Foundry also invites the community to actively participate in the arts. Educational programs are available to the public at all levels (adult, children, schools) as well as art classes. Summer camps in various art media and theater are available for preschool through ninth grades in June and July. Individual artists also offer classes. There is an adult book club meeting once a month and a children's book club. There are also one-day events offered throughout the year such as the Mommy and Me Nutcracker Tea in November for holiday fun. For more information on class and event schedules, please contact the Foundry. Admission to view the galleries is free, and memberships are also available.

Tuesday through Thursday, 10 a.m.–8 p.m.
Friday and Saturday, 10 a.m.–5 p.m.
Sunday, noon–4 p.m.
Closed Monday
(636) 255-0270
520 N Main Center
www.foundryartcentre.org

AMERISTAR CASINO RESORT & SPA

As the number one attraction in St. Charles County, Ameristar Casino boasts 130,000 square feet of the latest and most popular table games, slots, and video poker along with a live poker room. Late night and early morning snackers can order pizza, subs, salads, and more at the Casino Bar Deli (open 11 a.m. to 6 a.m.) while LIXX bar keeps your favorite cocktails coming.

    Non-gamblers will be delighted to know that there are numerous other reasons to visit Ameristar Casino. The restaurants alone offer big variety with a little something for everyone. The Falcon Diner is open for breakfast, lunch, and dinner. Guests can't lose with the signature chicken fried steak, a hand-scooped milkshake, or even the pot roast. Drool-worthy desserts hypnotize you from behind the glass case at the Bakery, where even whole pies can be purchased. At the casual Amerisports Bar & Grill you'll find typical bar food and plenty of TVs for sports lovers. Reservations are recommended for fine dining at Bugatti's Steak & Pasta, which specializes in Italian cuisine, seafood, and the finest steaks. Seafood lovers should indulge at Pearl's Oyster Bar where creole, cajun, and Asian flavors dominate the menu. For big appetites, the Landmark Buffet is open for lunch and dinner and features interactive display cooking stations. Numerous dining experiences are available including the Champagne Brunch and the newly added Steak and Ale package. Prices are discounted for ages 4–10 years, while kids 3 and under are free everyday. The swanky King Cat Club is a 1950s-inspired lounge and martini bar that serves appetizers upon request.

    For entertainment, the Bottleneck Blues Bar showcases local musicians and has hosted longtime favorites such as the Little River Band and Bret Michaels. There's an arcade for kids and a cute gift shop worth stopping in near the indoor fountain at the main entrance. No matter what time of day, you're sure to find gazers mesmerized by the ever rising and falling water, along with those posing for the perfect camera shot with the fountain as their backdrop.

As the first AAA Four Diamond hotel in St. Charles, Ameristar Casino Resort & Spa offers modern and inviting luxury suites with sunken living rooms, floor-to-ceiling windows bestowing Missouri River and city views, oversized baths, and two TVs. The 1,900-square-foot Presidential Suite is ideal for travelers looking for a grand overnight stay. Boasting a state-of-the-art surround sound system, numerous TVs, a custom pool table, kitchen, wet bar, large sitting area with a two-way fireplace, a spa bath, additional guest bath, and spectacular views of the St. Louis skyline, the Presidential Suite is perfect for entertaining your own party or just relaxing. You'll have everything you need without ever leaving your room.

Hotel guests and visitors alike can indulge in some much needed relaxation at the blissful Ara Spa. For the ultimate in pampering, schedule a massage, nail, or skin therapy session. The splash package is free with any 50 minute or longer spa service and includes the sauna, Swiss shower, steam, and hydro pools designed to stimulate circulation and relieve muscle tension. "Splash at Ara" can be purchased separately from $30 to $50, depending on the day of the week, to melt away worries and stress. In addition, the package offers access to the indoor and outdoor pools (complete with a fire pit) and hot tubs too. Guests of the hotel can also utilize the fitness center 24 hours a day.

With all wants and needs under one roof, Ameristar Casino Resort & Spa has also become a popular choice for conferences, weddings, and private parties. The Discovery Ballroom is quite elegant and spacious, while Home offers a trendy club atmosphere for private celebrations. Conveniently, self and valet (don't forget to tip) parking is free. For all things Ameristar, visit the website.

(636) 949-7777
1 Ameristar Boulevard
www.ameristar.com.

FOR THE ROMANTIC

CENTENNIAL CARRIAGE RIDES
Centennial Carriage Rides offers evening horse-drawn carriage rides on historic Main Street. The carriages are also available for special events such as weddings.

(636) 398-4123
875 Foristell Road, Wentzville
laura@centennialcarriage.com
www.centennialcarriage.com

THE CONSERVATORY
For a garden wedding any time of the year, choose the Conservatory, a tropical glass garden house. Beautiful gardens inside and out make a lovely setting for "I do's" as well as beautiful photos. Main Street itself offers further photo ops for that special day. The Conservatory also provides many amenities for brides and grooms. Visit every Wednesday for an open house, 10:30 a.m.–8 p.m.

(636) 947-0414
1001 S Main St.
ido@gardenwedding.com
www.gardenwedding.com

GRAND OPERA HOUSE AND BANQUET CENTER

With its history as an opulent theater and opera house, this may be the perfect venue for your wedding or other special event. Originally built circa 1870–1880 (historians differ on the date), the theater was on the second floor and a dry goods business on the first. The opera house was accessed on Main Street by ascending a beautiful staircase to the second floor ticket office and 350-seat theater. The building was destroyed by fire in 1881 and rebuilt. Today, the Grand Opera House hosts events of your choosing for 50 to 200 guests. For the first time in many years, there are also theater events available (see website for information).

(314) 406-3783
311 N Main St.
www.ohbanquets.com

OLD STONE CHAPEL AND BANQUET CENTER

The Old Stone Chapel and Banquet Center offers a site for both weddings and banquets in one location. The center is also available for meetings and events.

(636) 947-8270
1106 S Main St.
www.oldstonechapel.com

Another Amazing Wedding and Reception Site
by
HSC Ballrooms!

Old Stone Chapel

For more information and to book an event call 636.947.8270 or visit wwww.oldstonechapel.com

FOR THE FITNESS BUFF

BLUE BIRD YOGA
Blue Bird Yoga studio moved to Main Street with the intention of bringing the blue bird of happiness and health to the area. The studio offers sessions in hatha and vinyasa yoga with a schedule to meet anyone's needs. Classes run from early in the morning until evening. See the time and fee schedule on the website.

(636) 493-9293
416 S Main St.
www.bluebirdyoga.com

MAIN STREET GYM
Main Street Gym offers a myriad of options to help you stay fit—top-notch equipment, classes, personal trainers, and more.

Monday through Thursday, 5 a.m.–8 p.m.
Friday, 5 a.m.–7 p.m.
Saturday and Sunday, 8 a.m.–1 p.m.
(636) 946-4100
334 N Main St.
www.mainstreetgym.com

STEEL SHOP TENNIS CLUB
The Steel Shop Tennis Club is the first new tennis club in the St. Louis area in 30 years. The club is located in a building that once housed American Car and Foundry, a company that built train cars. There are five courts and three hitting alleys, built to make the tennis experience most enjoyable. The club hosts leagues, clinics, private lessons, and team practices for both juniors and adults. There is also a snack bar available.

Monday through Thursday, 8 a.m.–10 p.m.
Friday and Saturday, 8 a.m.–8 p.m. (Please call ahead.)
(636) 916-1400
900 N Main St.
www.steelshoptennisclub.com

FOR THE GHOST HUNTER

ST. CHARLES GHOST TOURS
The gaslights flicker, leaves rustle, and footsteps echo on cobbled streets, setting the perfect scene for Dr. Michael Henry to lead a group of ghost hunters along South Main Street. For eight years, Dr. Henry has been entertaining visitors and residents alike with his tour of some of the most haunted locations on South Main Street. The tour visits a darkened alley in the 300 block of the street where the spirit of a former St. Charles sheriff bemoans his participation in the hanging of criminals who may not have been guilty. At a bar on the banks of Blanchette Creek, the audience listens for the ghostly cry of a cat as it is thrown toward the waters by a group of bullies. The death of that cat perhaps led to the tragic suicide of its young hearing-impaired owner, who also haunts the area. These and many other tales pepper the trek down Main Street.

Dr. Henry researches each story in a number of ways before adding it to the tour. He begins with the oral stories passed from one person to another, then proceeds to look for historical facts to back up the tales, including letters, diaries, and newspaper accounts. One of his favorite ghosts is one to whom he has a personal connection, the "lady in white," who reportedly roams Main Street in her wedding gown. One of Henry's ancestors, Hiram Berry, speaks fondly of said lady in a letter he wrote as he left town because of some trouble he encountered. Does the trouble have anything to do with his affection for the lady in white? Dr. Henry also uses equipment designed to detect paranormal activity during the tours. Participants are encouraged to bring their cameras to capture ghostly movements for themselves.

Dr. Henry is the author of *Ghosts of St. Charles.*

Tours are scheduled for Friday and Saturday at 7 p.m., 9:30 p.m., and midnight (if demand allows). Because of the nature of the tours, Dr. Henry recommends ages 14 and above only. Cost is $20 and reservations are required. Keep in mind that tours fill quickly. Special group tours for six or more people may also be arranged. Call Dr. Michael Henry for reservations.

(314) 374-6102
info@stcharlesghosts.com
www.stcharlesghosts.com

FESTIVALS/EVENTS

CHRISTMAS TRADITIONS

The biggest festival of the year on historic Main Street brings thousands of visitors who take a step back in time and celebrate the Christmas holidays in a very special way. Christmas Traditions begins on the Friday after Thanksgiving when Santa arrives in St. Charles. It continues on Wednesday and Friday evenings and all day Saturday and Sunday until Christmas Eve, when all the special characters return to their magical homes, leaving behind a glow of happiness on the faces of all the children and children at heart who have visited Christmas Traditions. The festival features "Christmas Legends" from history, stories, and folklore, and each one has his or her own trading card that visitors love to collect. Of course the most important legend of all, Santa, along with his lovely wife, Mrs. Claus, are in residence at the KATY Depot in Frontier Park to visit with children at specified times. Characters travel up and down Main Street, interacting and posing for photos with people who are enchanted by them. Each year new characters and events are added. Carolers add a touch of music to the atmosphere. There are roasted chestnuts and toasted marshmallows (on Friday night at the Missouri State Capitol) as well as sing-a-longs at the Gazebo (on Sunday). And at the end of each evening the characters parade in candlelight to Bertholdt Park and lead everyone in song.

In 2014, the inaugural Kristkindlmarkt, a traditional German Christmas market, was held at the Lewis and Clark Boat House the weekend after Thanksgiving. The market offers traditionally German items such as ornaments, nutcrackers, cuckoo clocks, and beer steins as well as toys, jewelry, clothes, home décor, and more. Also available are German pastries and special hot chocolate in a souvenir cup shaped like a boot. Admission is free.

230 S Main St.
Historic Main Street
www.historicstcharles.com/things-to-do/Christmas-Traditions

kids

FARMERS MARKET
Visit the Farmers Market in the Foundry parking lot at the north end of Riverside Drive, 7 a.m.–noon on Saturday morning, May 15 through October 30.

www.rendezvousinstcharles.com/farmersmarket.html

FESTIVAL OF THE LITTLE HILLS (FETES DES PETITE CÔTES)
The name of this annual craft festival pays homage to the early name given St. Charles by French settlers—Les Petites Côtes, or "the Little Hills." It is one

of the city's largest events and has been voted "Best Craft Fair in the Midwest" by *Midwest Living* magazine. The festival is held the third full weekend of August each year along historic Main Street and in Frontier Park. It features craft vendors, specialty foods, and entertainment. Applications for vendor space are available in January.

(636) 940-0095
P.O. Box 1323
info@festivalofthelittlehills.com
www.festivalofthelittlehills.com

FÊTE DE GLACE

Held each January on North Main Street, Fête de Glace offers a fun winter activity as ice carvers create sparkling creations from start to finish out of a 260-pound block of ice. The event is a competition among carvers from the region and includes a people's choice award. Admission is free.

www.historicstcharles.com/includes/events/Fete-de-Glace-Ice-Carving-Competition

FRONTIER PARK

Frontier Park sits on the banks of the Missouri River in the heart of historic St. Charles. It is the location for many of the festivals and special events held throughout the year. It is also where you will find the picturesque Katy Depot, restored and moved from its original location at the foot of Tompkins Street. Historically, the depot was the site of an infamous robbery and kidnapping in 1921. Five men robbed a U.S. mail messenger of $110,000 that was headed for five St. Charles banks and kidnapped the carrier. The man escaped but the money was lost.

The park is also the site of a performance stage and host to a portion of the Katy Trail. A favorite photo opportunity is the 15-foot statue of Lewis

and Clark with their dog, Seaman. In the summer, a variety of food trucks line up on select evenings and diners are entertained with live music. Admission is free.

500 S Riverside Dr.
www.stcharlesparks.com/143/parks/frontier-park.php

THE GAZEBO IN KISTER PARK
Located in Kister Park in the heart of historic Main Street, the gazebo offers a perfect photo opportunity. A Kissing Ball is hung during Christmas Traditions, and the site has served as the location of more than one marriage proposal for the romantically minded. It is also a popular spot for wedding photos. The official name is the Albert F. Kister Park and Bandstand, but you can call it the Gazebo.

400 S Main St.

GREATER ST. CHARLES CONVENTION & VISITORS BUREAU
The Greater St. Charles Convention & Visitors Bureau (GSCCVB) is located in the heart of the historic district. Friendly staff and volunteers are available to help visitors plan their trips to the city with maps, information, and even coupons for local businesses. For bigger events such as conventions, meetings, tours, and sporting events, the bureau provides extensive convention services.

Monday through Friday, 8 a.m.–5 p.m.; Saturday, 10 a.m.–5 p.m.;
Sunday, noon–5 p.m.
(636) 946-7776
(800) 366-2427
230 S Main St.
www.historicstcharles.com

KATY TRAIL STATE PARK

The Katy Trail State Park is the longest rail trail in the United States. It follows the former right-of-way of the Missouri-Kansas-Texas Railroad from Clinton to Machens (passing through St. Charles) for 240 miles. When the Katy Railroad ceased operations in 1986, the Missouri Department of Natural Resources began acquiring right-of-way to create the trail, helped by legislation and donations. The trail mostly follows the Missouri River and is a haven for hikers, joggers, cyclists, nature lovers, and history buffs. The landscape varies from wetlands to open prairie, and history can be found in the small railroad towns the trail passes through as well as in the Missouri Rhineland, where German settlers came in the mid-1800s. Many of the communities along the trail welcome visitors with amenities. Admission is free.

www.mostateparks.com/park/katy-trail-state-park

LEWIS & CLARK FIFE AND DRUM CORPS

The Lewis & Clark Fife and Drum Corps is made up of young people aged 9–17 years. It is an opportunity to learn to play fife or drum and become a musician in the corps or to learn military bearing as a member of the color guard. The corps was formed by the late John Dengler and the South Main Preservation Society in 1992 to share and promote the history of the Lewis and Clark expedition and the city of St. Charles. The youngsters perform locally and across the United States. They are the host fife and drum corps for the annual Lewis and Clark Heritage Days in St. Charles. The corps is often in residence, marching down Main Street and attending many of the festivals and special events the city hosts. The uniform is the dress uniform of field musicians and color guard from the 1st U.S. Infantry, circa 1804–1810. The red coats worn by the musicians are sometimes thought to be British uniforms, but it was traditional for musicians to wear opposite colors on the battlefield to increase their visibility. The color guard wears the traditional blue coat with red trim. There is a weekly practice with free fife and drum instruction. Other costs are nominal.

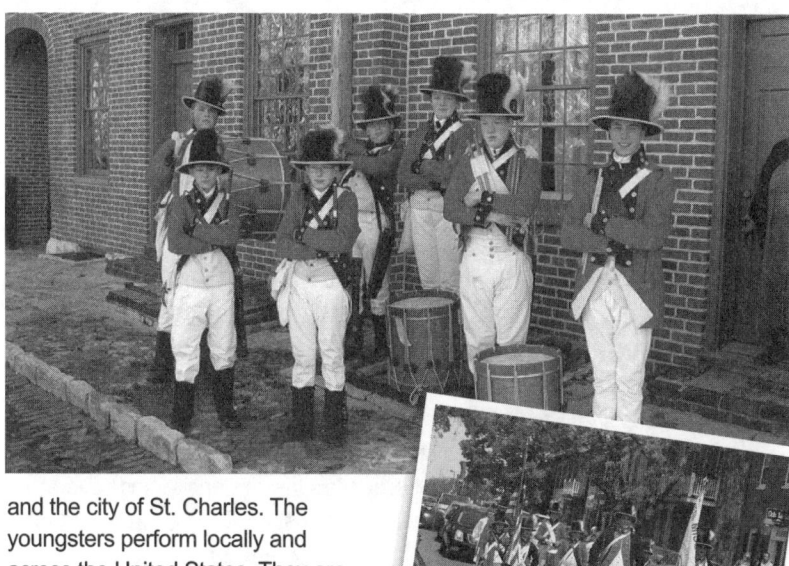

lewisandclarkfdc@gmail.com
www.lewisandclarkfifeanddrum.com

LEWIS AND CLARK HERITAGE DAYS

Lewis and Clark Heritage Days is an annual event commemorating the meet-up of Lewis and Clark in St. Charles before they set out on their voyage of discovery up the Missouri River. Heritage Days was first held in 1979 and has been held each year since on the third weekend in May in Frontier Park. Events include a parade, musket and cannon demonstrations, a skillet throw, and period music, food, and wares. The Discovery Expedition of St. Charles provides a living history exhibit with their military encampment in the park, while the Lewis and Clark Fife and Drum Corps hosts a fife and drum corps muster.

www.lewisandclarkheritagedays.com

MISSOURI RIVER IRISH FEST

The Missouri River Irish Fest is the largest free Irish festival in the St. Louis region. The group seeks to promote Irish culture, music, and dance as well as raise funds for the Irish Chapter of the St. Charles Sister Cities Programs, Inc. Cardonagh, Donegal, Ireland, is St. Charles's Irish sister city, and several successful student exchanges have been accomplished. The Children's Village is a popular event during the festival.

www.moriveririshfest.com

MISSOURI TARTAN DAY FESTIVITIES

Missouri Tartan Day Festivities celebrate Scottish-American culture. Festivalgoers can enjoy music, dance, food, athletics, storytelling, education, and various interactive events.

The purpose is to emphasize the existing and historical links between Scotland and those of Scottish descent now living in North America.

April 6 is the traditional date for Tartan Day Festivities, the anniversary of the Declaration of Arbroath declaring Scotland's independence and its right to defend itself against unjust attacks. The declaration was sent to Pope John XXII on April 6, 1320.

One of the highlights of the festivities is the Clan Village, which features displays and histories of various Scottish clans. The event is held in Frontier Park, weather permitting. Festivities are free and open to the public.

P.O. Box 1961
Info@motartanday.com
www.motartanday.com

kids

MOSAICS MISSOURI FESTIVAL FOR THE ARTS
In 1992, the MOSAICS Art Festival Association was established to create and foster diversity and vitality of the arts and to broaden the availability, education, participation, and appreciation of the arts throughout the community. The festival is held the second weekend of September each year.

MOSAICS is free and family friendly and offers artwork from approximately 100 juried artists from Missouri and surrounding states. The association strives to present a diversity of art work from artists working in a variety of media and with different experience levels. Admission is free.

(314) 482-5476
North Main St.
P.O. Box 1649
www.stcharlesmosaics.org

kids

MUSIC ON MAIN
Come on down to the 100–200 blocks of North Main Street the third Wednesday of the month, May through September, 5 p.m.–7:30 p.m., for a free outdoor concert. Food and drink are available for purchase.

www.historicstcharles.com/includes/events/Music-on-Main

OKTOBERFEST
The big question about Oktoberfest is, why is it in September? The answer lies not in St. Charles, Missouri, but in distant Munich, Germany. The first Oktoberfest was held the first week in October 1810 in Munich to celebrate the marriage of Crown Prince Ludwig and Princess Therese. Over the years the festival expanded to cover several weeks, and because of the cooling temperatures as October approaches, the festival was pushed back to September.

In St. Charles, the event combines food, vendors (offering authentic German goods), beer, fun events, games, and contests, with the opportunity to contribute to local charities. The 5K Rootbeer Run benefits Disabled Athlete Sports and there is a JDRF Walk to Cure Diabetes. The Kid's Zone donates the $5 admission fee to KEEN, an organization providing recreation programs for special needs children. A Wiener Takes All wiener dog derby for dachshunds includes races, a talent show, and a fashion show. On South Main Street, view the Antique Car Show with vehicles from 1989 and earlier. And participate in the Sam Adams Raise the Stein contest to see who hoists a full liter stein of beer longest or the Swiss Meats Brat Eating Contest to see which wurst eater is best.

Some events have an admission charge.

Frontier Park
222 S Riverside Dr.
www.stcharlesoktoberfest.com

RIVERFEST
Riverfest is St. Charles's annual Fourth of July celebration. The event kicks off with a Main Street parade and then moves to Frontier Park, where food and craft vendors ply their wares. The culmination is a brilliant fireworks display along the banks of the Missouri River. Admission is free.

Frontier Park
222 S Riverside Dr.
www.historicstcharles.com/includes/events/Riverfest

ST. CHARLES MUNICIPAL BAND CONCERTS
There has been a St. Charles band performing free public concerts in the city since 1819. The first was La Frenier Chauvin, a family band, that performed in a small park at 624 S. Main Street. In the 1830s, the Town Band played on Sunday afternoons at the Market House. Other town bands went under the names of the French Band, the German Band, and the St. Charles Brass Band. It is to that last group that a direct link can be found dating from 1870 to today's St. Charles Municipal Band.

The St. Charles Brass Band changed its name to the St. Charles Cornet Band and in 1897 performed concerts on Office Clerk's Hill (near the courthouse). After a few more name changes, that band became the

St. Charles Municipal Band in 1929. It was supported by a small tax levy and had a permanent director. Concerts were held in Blanchette Park until 1987, when they moved permanently to Frontier Park.

In 1992, the city eliminated funding to the band and they became a not-for-profit organization. The St. Charles Big Band is also a part of the St. Charles Municipal Band. Today they perform a series of summer concerts at the Jaycee Pavilion. Admission is free.

Frontier Park
222 S Riverside Dr.
www.stcharlesband.com

TRICK OR TREAT ON MAIN STREET

Each October 31 (or the closest weekday to Halloween), trick-or-treaters age 12 and under are invited to don their costumes and come to historic Main Street to collect treats. The event lasts from 3 p.m. to 5 p.m., as a solid line of children (and parents) parade down each side of the street tricking local store owners into giving out treats. One storekeeper reports giving out approximately 1,500 Tootsie Rolls! Admission is free.

Historic Main St.

kids

TEN MOST FREQUENTLY ASKED QUESTIONS FROM THE GSCCVB

1. WHERE'S THE RESTROOM?
Many businesses do not have public restrooms, but there are facilities in the Tourism Center, under the Gazebo in Kister Park, in the parking lot between McDonough and Water Streets, and between North Main and Riverside on Washington Street. The helpful map and brochure available from the Tourism Center has bathroom facilities marked.

2. I'M HUNGRY . . . ANY SUGGESTIONS FOR A GOOD PLACE TO EAT?
So many restaurants, so little time! Check the GSCCVB brochure for a list of restaurants. One is sure to feature the type of food you're looking for.

3. IS THE TOURISM CENTER A GIFT SHOP?
We are looking for souvenirs. This isn't a gift shop but there are numerous shops on the street that sell postcards and souvenirs.

4. DO YOU HAVE A CALENDAR OF EVENTS?
Take a look at that helpful GSCCVB brochure or visit our website at www.historicstcharles.com.

5. HOW OLD ARE THE BUILDINGS ALONG MAIN STREET?
Some of the buildings on the street date to the late 18th century, and many were built in the early 19th century. Many have plaques with historical information mounted on the outside of the building, or you can step inside and ask a friendly shopkeeper. The self-guided audio tour offered by GSCCVB (free) will also tell you lots about the buildings and dates.

6. WHERE'S THE FIRST MISSOURI STATE CAPITOL AND WHY DID IT MOVE TO JEFFERSON CITY?
The capitol is located at 200 S. Main Street. It was always meant to be a temporary location while the legislature sought a more central site in the state.

7. WHERE'S THE LEWIS & CLARK INFO—IS THERE A MUSEUM OR MONUMENT TO THEM?
Please visit the Lewis and Clark Boat House and Nature Center at 1050 S. Riverside Drive to find out all you could hope to know about Lewis and Clark. There is also a statue in Frontier Park that is a great place to take a picture.

8. WHERE CAN WE PARK OUR CAR?
Free parking is available on the street, in parking lots along Riverside Drive, between Water and McDonough Streets, and for a fee, in the public parking garage (enter off Monroe Street). Some spots are limited by time, and exceeding that time limit may result in a parking ticket. Parking is marked in the handy-dandy GSCCVB brochure.

9. WHY DOES THE RIVER FLOW NORTH (UPSTREAM)?
The Missouri River is the longest river in North America. From its source in western Montana, it flows east and south to meet up with the Mississippi River. Its northward flow through St. Charles is part of its ultimate journey eastward to the Mississippi.

10. HOW FAR FROM HERE IS THE CASINO?
The casino is located a short distance south of the Tourism Center, right off Main Street, at 1 Ameristar Boulevard.

Thanks to Pam Schulz of the Greater St. Charles Convention and Visitors Bureau for her help with this section!

ST. CHARLES NEIGHBORHOODS – FRENCHTOWN

FRENCHTOWN

The Frenchtown Historic District is one of three areas of St. Charles on the National Register of Historic Places. The area was settled by the French in the late 1700s and early 1800s, as more people moved into the city of St. Charles and the South Main area became too crowded for, among other things, the gardens many settlers wanted to cultivate. The homes had a common floor plan with a raised basement, two rooms wide and one room deep, and outside exits from both rooms. This style of architecture is visible today in many of the historic homes that grace the area. Germans, who came to St. Charles in the mid-1800s, turned many of the log structures into brick cottages and developed a strong business presence in the area, a virtual city within a city.

The area is working to revitalize and has a number of retail shops with an emphasis on antiques.

A SHABBY ROAD
There are eight gallery spaces in this delightful shop featuring vintage items, repurposed and painted furniture, and home décor items.

Wednesday through Saturday,
10 a.m.–4 p.m.
Sunday, noon–4 p.m.
(636) 206-5007
913 N Second St.
ashabbyroad@yahoo.com

THE ATELIER AT FRENCHTOWN/RED DOOR FURNITURE COMPANY
The Atelier is a monthly collective of local artists and vintage curators presented by Red Door Furniture Company. The market features art, handmade items, and carefully chosen vintage finds. Current vendors include the Vintage Peddlers, My Vintage Varia, Meldt Vintage, Giggle Poo, Buddha Body and Bath, and more. The Red Door also has a second location in Fox & Hound Antiques on Main Street. The Main Street location offers handcrafted and restyled one-of-a-kind furniture pieces. Their Signature Tables are created from reclaimed doors or windows with a coat of red paint on the bottom. The store offers a selection of jewelry and gifts as well as selling Miss Mustard Seed's Milk Paint. Check their website for information on workshops that teach customers to use milk paint.

Open the first weekend of each month
Friday and Saturday, 10 a.m.–5 p.m.
Sunday, noon–4 p.m.
Or by appointment
(314) 779-8428
1105 N Second St.
In Fox & Hound Antiques at 604 South Main Street, Wednesday through Saturday, 11 a.m.–5 p.m. Sunday, noon–4 p.m.
www.reddoorfurnitureco.com

BARTON BROTHERS ANTIQUES

This family owned business specializes in woodworking, re-gluing, furniture stripping, furniture repair, furniture refinishing, chair repair and refinishing, antique restoration, antique repair, and antique refinishing. The showroom also offers restored furniture for sale.

Monday through Friday, 9 a.m.–5 p.m.
Saturday, 10 a.m.–5 p.m.
(636) 399-5295
820 N Second St.
sbbarton0811@att.net
www.bartonsantiques.net

BAYARD STREET ANTIQUE MALL

Four rooms and 24 vendors join together to offer all vintage (1970s and before) items. The rooms and displays are decorated in a manner to give customers ideas to take home and use.

Tuesday through Saturday,
10 a.m.–5 p.m.
(636) 925-0292
1200 N Second St.
bayardstreetantiques@gmail.com

BEAU MONDE BRIDAL/WEDDING GALLERY

This bridal and special occasion salon offers personal attention from a trained staff to help make wedding and special days perfect.

Monday, Wednesday, Thursday, Friday, 11 a.m.–6 p.m.
Saturday, 11 a.m.–5 p.m.
Sunday, noon–4 p.m.
Appointments only for bridal salons; walk-ins welcome to special-occasion salons
(636) 573-9022 for Beau Monde Bridal
(636) 724-9012 for Wedding Gallery
801 N Second St.
www.beaumondebridal.com
www.weddinggalleryweb.com

FRENCH CONNECTION ANTIQUES

French Connection has been open longer than any other shop in Frenchtown, family owned and operated since 1982. They offer high-end antique furniture from circa 1850 to the 1930s, as well as refinishing and repair, lighting, and lamp and fixture wiring.

(636) 947-7044
826 N Second St.
www.rubylane.com/shop/frenchconnectionantiques

FRENCHTOWN ANTIQUE MALL & COLLECTIBLES

The largest antique mall in Frenchtown offers a wide variety of items including linens, vinyl records, furniture, fishing collectibles, knickknacks, gifts, glassware, jewelry, and more.

Open seven days a week, 10 a.m.–5 p.m.
(636) 724-0261
1513A N Second St.

THE FRENCHTOWN HERITAGE MUSEUM AND RESEARCH CENTER

Today Frenchtown is anchored by the Frenchtown Heritage Museum and Research Center. The museum is housed in a former firehouse dating to circa 1880. Exhibits rotate and include an annual quilt show. The main exhibit area, where exhibits are changed regularly, boasts a restored, circa-1850 horse-drawn hook and ladder fire wagon. Photos capturing the building's history and that of St. Charles Borromeo, Academy of the Sacred Heart, and the American Car Foundry are displayed. In the Garden Room, a model of St. Charles in the early 1900s and one of Old Borromeo Church are displayed, along with displays and photos of Frenchtown architecture and businesses. A meeting room is available as well as a small research library. The backyard is home to a 1929 caboose manufactured by American Car and Foundry, where, when restored, educational programs will be held. The museum also hosts a Christmas train display. Admission is free, but donations are appreciated.

Wednesday through Saturday,
noon–3 p.m. and by appointment
Admission is free, donations appreciated.
(636) 724-2106
1121 N Second St.
info@frenchtownmuseum.com
www.frenchtownmuseum.com

LIL' SHOPPE OF TREASURES
Located in a small house, this shop features an eclectic array of vintage items.

Hours vary.
(314) 814-6184
1218 N Second St.
lilshoppeoftreasures@gmail.com

SECONDHAND CHIC MARKETPLACE
A mecca for shoppers and decorators featuring slightly worn home décor. CASH ONLY.

Open the first weekend of each month
Friday, 10 a.m.–5 p.m.
Saturday and Sunday, 10 a.m.–4 p.m.
(314) 378-4633
910 N Second St.
foxanne@secondhandchicmarketplace.com
www.secondhandchicmarketplace.com

WHITE TRADITIONS BRIDAL HOUSE
This small shop offers a selection of designer bridal gowns, accessories, bridesmaid dresses, and tuxedos for the groom along with personal attention for each bride.

Tuesday, Wednesday, Thursday,
11 a.m.–7 p.m.
Friday and Saturday, 10 a.m.–4 p.m.

Please call for an appointment.
(636) 939-6005
827 N Second St.
whitetraditions@gmail.com
www.whitetraditionsbridal.com

WORN VINTAGE
The ladies at Worn Vintage are first and foremost stylists. They carry an inventory of vintage items available for rental to make any event or home special, and they offer the wherewithal to carry it out with no stress for the customer.

(314) 323-1131
825 N Second St.
wornvintagerental@hotmail.com
www.wornvintagestl.com

PLACES TO STAY

BITTERSWEET INN
Located in the Frenchtown Historic District, the Bittersweet Inn is an elegantly restored home dating to 1864 that typifies the architecture the district is known for. There are three bedrooms and two suites offered as well as charming outdoor garden areas. A homemade gourmet breakfast is included. The inn is a short distance from Main Street attractions and the innkeeper is willing to help plan special activities such as a spa day or restaurant reservations for guests.

(636) 724-7778
1101 N Third St.
bittersweetinn@yahoo.com
www.bittersweetinn.com

L'AUBERGE ST. CHARLES GUEST HOUSE
Stay in this restored 1868 Second Empire home within walking distance of Main Street. With the restoration, the house combines the historic with modern comfort and amenities. There are three bedrooms and two baths with a maximum occupancy of six.

(636) 288-3363
1411 N Second St.
www.stcharlesvacation.com

LOCOCO HOUSE II AND III
Recently Lococo House III changed from a traditional bed and breakfast to a guest house that features three bedrooms, one bath, a kitchen, and a living room area. The purpose is to provide a family-like housing alternative to visitors at a reasonable price.

Lococo House II continues as a traditional bed and breakfast with overnight accommodations including a full breakfast.

The friendly staff at Lococo House will also arrange van service to and from the Katy Trail and Main Street as well as Girls' Night Out activities and other tours of the area.

(636) 946-0619
Lococo House II
1309 N Fifth St.
Lococo House III
1307 N Fifth St.
rhonaloc@charter.net
www.lococohouse.com

SUNDERMEIER RV PARK

The park location began as the family farm 60 years ago. After World War II the farm was incorporated into the city limits, and to help meet a housing shortage it became a mobile home park. Today it is a five-star, award-winning RV park. The park offers 106 sites with concrete pads and full hook-ups as well as 10 sleeping cottages. Some cottages are deluxe with electric fireplaces and kitchens, sleeping one to four people; others are simple sleeping cottages for one to four guests. All cottages have air conditioning, heat, and private baths. The park also has restrooms, laundry facilities, and Wi-Fi. There is an event room available for rental as well as a general store with RV supplies, snacks, and gifts. The park is open year-round.

(800) 929-0832
111 Transit St.
info@sundermeierrvpark.com
www.sundermeierrvpark.com

THE SHRINE OF ST. ROSE PHILIPPINE DUCHESNE

Visitors come from all over the world bringing petitions and prayers to the pioneer known for her kindness and perseverance. Duchesne (meaning "of oak" in French) was quite a fitting name for the woman whose prayer life was ever strong and led such a courageous life for a woman of her time. Born in Grenoble, France, in 1769, St. Rose Philippine Duchesne was already in her late forties by the time she came to America, where she opened the first free school west of the Mississippi in 1818. The Academy of the Sacred Heart is now a thriving elementary school. Despite harsh conditions, she sought out her longtime dream of living among the Native Americans as a teacher and advocate. Mother Duchesne spent her final years at the Academy in St. Charles before dying in 1852. She was canonized in 1988 by Pope John Paul II. After being moved several times upon the property, her remains finally rest within the shrine built in her honor. Artist William Schickel designed a modern interior using granite in the sanctuary to reflect the hard life that Philippine Duchesne lived on the grounds. The shrine is open daily from 9 a.m. to 4 p.m. with no appointment necessary. However, to fully feel the presence of St. Rose Philippine Duchesne, visit during docent hours on Tuesday, Thursday, and Friday (9 a.m.–11 a.m. and 1 p.m.–3 p.m.), the first and third Saturday of each month (10 a.m.–noon and 1 p.m.–3 p.m.), and the first and third Sunday (noon–3 p.m.) for a full tour. Large groups should make reservations by calling the shrine director. Due to future construction, the main entrance of the property will be moving and visitors are directed to follow signage to the shrine. Keep in mind that students will be present when school is in session so a summer visit might be more suitable. However, many like to pay respect on November 18th, St. Philippine's feast day. In addition to the shrine, those on tour with a docent will see parlors of the early convent building, areas where she spent her time, where she died at age 82, and relics of the original convent including items handmade by Mother Duchesne and books that she and her fellow missionaries brought with them from France in the early 1800s. Be sure to sign the guest registry in the shrine. Admission is free, but donations are appreciated.

(636) 946-6127, x1801
619 N Second St., St. Charles
www.duchesneshrine.org

ST. CHARLES NEIGHBORHOODS – CENTRAL

ST. CHARLES

The perfect mix of both old and new, St. Charles City is a thriving suburban community ideally located near interstates, the Missouri and Mississippi Rivers, and the Lambert–St. Louis International Airport. While home to more than 65,000 residents, in addition to numerous national and regional businesses, the city maintains a friendly small town feel and welcomes tourists from all over the world, including visitors from sister city Ludwigsburg, Germany.

Voted Best Casino in *AAA Midwest Traveler* magazine's list of Best Places, Ameristar Casino is the largest draw to the city. Lindenwood University currently educates students from over 100 countries, with its main campus located in St. Charles on 500 sprawling acres. Lindenwood's J. Scheidegger Center for the Arts, the Foundry Arts Centre, the Family Arena, and the St. Charles Convention Center host countless events year-round and lend to a bustling arts and entertainment program, while Bass Pro is a popular family-friendly stop for free educational programs and activities.

While low crime rates, employment growth, and the low cost of living all contributed to the city of St. Charles landing on the list of "50 Best Cities to Live" by the *24/7 Wall St.* website, it is also a splendid place to visit. Bursting at the seams with a wide range of activities and a healthy offering of arts and entertainment, along with a wealth of history, it is unlike any other city in the county. It is the only community in the state of Missouri, including the St. Louis metropolitan region, to be on the list.

With its brick-lined streets, historic buildings, and nearby riverfront, Main Street is the true heart of St. Charles. It is the largest historic preservation district in Missouri, drawing over a million people each year. Its quaint, old-world charm captivates visitors with unique shops, one-of-a-kind restaurants, and enchanting places to stay. One can also see the first state capitol here, engage in an historical walking tour, or attend one of the city's popular festivals.

Divided into distinct neighborhoods, the Midtown Neighborhood Historic District of St. Charles City was recently named to the National Register of Historic Places by the National Park Service. This is considered a great honor and consists of a multiyear study of historical and architectural details. The county courthouse, numerous residences (including the Link House at 1005 Jefferson St.), churches, schools, and businesses are all located within the Midtown Neighborhood, with the earliest structure dating back to 1838. Romanesque Revival, Queen Anne, Federal, and Italianate, just to name a few, are architectural styles represented within the neighborhood.

St. Charles is a busy city, but an abundance of picturesque parks and green space also make it an outdoor haven. Numerous outdoor recreational opportunities such as fishing, swimming, and park programs exist, yet a constant favorite pastime is biking or hiking the Katy Trail, which winds along the riverfront in St. Charles and extends across the state. With something to offer all ages and interest groups, St. Charles City provides a piece of the past and present spectacularly wrapped into one.

SHOPPING

BASS PRO

In addition to carrying items for all things outdoor, Bass Pro entertains with wildlife displays, an 8,000-gallon aquarium where visitors can watch fish-feeding demos on Saturdays and Sundays, boat shows, and hunting and fishing classes. Kids can enroll in summer camp, groups can schedule tours, and well-behaved leashed pups can shop with their companions. The FREE PBR Family Event is great fun for adults and kids too! This event consists of bull roping, stick bull riding, face painting, and more. Don't forget the holidays . . . there's Santa's Wonderland, an Easter Egg Hunt, and Halloween haunting too. For educational fun for the whole family, including your dog, visit Bass Pro 364 days a year.

Monday through Saturday, 9 a.m.–9 p.m.
Sunday, 10 a.m.–7 p.m.
(636) 688-2500
1365 S. Fifth St.
www.basspro.com

kids

COMIC BOOK RELIEF

Shoppers will find a large selection of current and back issues of comic books, toys, games, supplies, and graphic novels. Customers can pre-order items and get a sneak peak at products soon to arrive at the store. Find out how you can receive your freebie on Free Comic Book Day by logging on to the website.

Monday through Saturday,
11 a.m.–7 p.m.
Sunday, noon–6 p.m.
(636) 940-1244
2224 N 3rd St.
www.comicbookrelief.com

ROEMER ORIGINALS

Specializing in custom-created and hand-carved jewelry, including wedding bands, Roemer Originals is known for quality, unique designs, and one-of-a-kind pieces. Whether you're in the market for something new or want to reinvent a current piece, Roemer Originals provides trustworthy and attentive service. View photos of some of their breathtaking creations on the website and call for appointments outside regular hours.

(636) 947-7207
1163 First Capitol Dr.
www.roemeroriginals.com

STEVE'S PRODUCE
Located behind Doozle's, this market is open daily during their selling season and offers fresh and reasonably priced produce, locally made honey, salsa, jams, plants, and more. In addition, customers can find seasonal merchandise like pumpkins, corn stalks, and Christmas trees at Steve's Produce. Go to Facebook or call for more information.

(636) 575-0592
3156 Elm Point Industrial Dr.
Find Steve's Produce on Facebook

VACCARO & SONS PRODUCE
For fresh fruit, vegetables, and chrysanthemums, in addition to locally produced goods like jams, pickled veggies, and dressings, visit Vaccaro & Sons. Open seasonally, customers can connect with Vaccaro & Sons on Facebook.

(636) 940-8505
739 S Duchesne Dr.

CONSIGNMENT AND RESALE

The hottest new trend right now actually involves everything old. Upcycling is all about repurposing, reinventing, and giving new life to items that are no longer wanted as they are. This is big business in the retail world with resale, DIY, and consignment shops cropping up all over town. Repurposed furniture, redesigned décor, and vintage items with a modern twist are commonly found in these types of stores, sometimes along with new merchandise. Find the perfect piece or just spend a few hours browsing unique buys at the following retailers.

DESIGN ON A DIME
Features new and gently used home décor and furniture. Offers custom painting of items already owned and purchased at the store. Prices reduced every 30 days.

(636) 949-5959
1982 Zumbehl Rd.
www.designonadimeconsign.com

DIFFERENT STUFF COLLECTIBLES
This shop features antiques, vintage items, and other unique merchandise. Hours are usually as listed, but call ahead just in case.

Closed Monday and Tuesday
Open Wednesday through Sunday,
10 a.m.–7 p.m.
(636) 233-0934
3502 N Hwy. 94
(use N 3rd St. for GPS)

GARVEY DÉCOR
Selling gently used home furnishings and accessories including shabby chic furniture. This resale shop touts resale prices instead of retail prices. Get a taste of what they offer on the website.

1 Garvey Pkwy., Ste. 100
www.garveydecor.com

GOOD BUY GIRLS
Carries new and used designer handbags, accessories, clothes, jewelry, home décor, and more. See pictures of new items on Facebook.

(636) 447-2077
4127 S Old Hwy. 94

I-70 SHOPPERS FAIR
This indoor/outdoor market has approximately 150 vendors.

Saturday and Sunday, 9 a.m.–4 p.m.
(636) 922-5900
4894 N Service Rd.

INSPIRED
Specializing in antique and vintage home décor and furniture with the use of Shabby Chic Paints. In addition to the main location, more merchandise is housed inside Secondhand Chic Marketplace on 2nd Street and Fox & Hound on Main Street. Find Inspired on Facebook.

(314) 374-0738
617 First Capitol Dr.
www.inspiredx3.com

MOVE IT ON & MORE
Find them on Facebook for current items of home décor and furniture.

Closed Sunday
(636) 724-3600
2031 Old Hwy. 94 S

RED POSIE VINTAGE RESALE
Specializes in vintage repurposed furniture and antiques. To sign up for workshops, see available items, read their blog, and

find other local places to shop for similar merchandise, visit the website.

Closed Monday
(314) 504-6385
At the corner of Fifth and McDonough
at 431 McDonough St.
www.redposie.com

ST. CHARLES ANTIQUE MALL
Voted the No. 1 antique mall in St. Charles County since opening in 1994. Shoppers will find 35,000 square feet of antiques, vintage pieces, and collectibles.

Open daily, 10 a.m.–6 p.m.
(636) 939-4178
3004 S St. Peters Pkwy., Ste. U
www.missouriantiquemalls.com

TREN-DEEZ VILLAGE
Customized shabby chic furniture, home décor, and more. Offers classes and will paint pieces that customers bring in. Visit them on Facebook for hours and pics of cute merchandise.

1522 Caulks Hill Rd.
Find Tren-DeeZ Village on Facebook

WISE OWL RESALE
A large clothing inventory along with jewelry, furniture, and household items. Visit the website for the deal of the week.

Monday through Saturday, 10 a.m.–6 p.m.
(636) 724-5722
301 Droste Rd.
www.wiseowlresale.com

RESTAURANTS/DINING

Monday through Saturday,
6 a.m.–4 p.m.
Sunday, 6 a.m.–2 p.m.
(636) 946-5556
130 N Kingshighway St.
Find Allin's Diner on Facebook

ALLIN'S DINER

The waitresses at Allin's Diner serve up huge portions of friendliness along with scrumptious eats, and rarely let your coffee get low before topping it off. A must-dine in St. Charles City, Allin's offers breakfast and lunch menu items and is family owned and operated. According to owner Dave, the homemade pancakes and the breakfast burrito made with chorizo sausage are among customers' favorites. Soups are a big deal at Allin's too! With around 80 current recipes, Chef Dave is always creating new blends and sharing them in his soup classes, which typically start in the fall. For $20 per person, you can make two kinds of soups and take them home with you. In addition, cold soup is always in stock to purchase for meals at home. Though the diner itself is small, tables open up quickly and there's counter seating too. The walls are lined with photos of frequent customers, and quirky facts adorn the tables for customers to enjoy during the short wait until orders arrive. Daily soups, timely information, and holiday hours are posted on Facebook. Lindenwood students receive a 10 percent discount with their student ID. Look for the eye-catching exterior and you won't miss it! Call to register for classes.

BAR LOUIE

With garage doors that open up to a good-sized patio complete with a fire pit, Bar Louie is a great choice for lunch, dinner, or just meeting friends for a drink while listening to some live music. One might expect Bar Louie to be a typical bar with the usual bar food, and indeed, guests will find sliders, sandwiches, and deliciously huge portions of salad on the menu. Yet there's a surprising variety of dishes one might not expect. Choices include sesame-encrusted ahi tuna, tacos, voodoo chicken, and baked mac & cheese (with the option to add chicken, shrimp, bacon, broccoli, or jalapeños). However, if you order only one thing, it must be the tots. Beware, they are so mouthwatering good that you can't eat just one!

(636) 669-0400
1650 Beale St., #180
www.barlouieamerica.com

CONCETTA'S

If you have ever wanted to be part of an Italian family, visit Concetta's Italian Restaurant. One of the goals of this establishment is to make guests feel exactly that way—a part of the family. The restaurant uses Arcobasso family recipes, giving diners an authentic Italian dining experience.

Monday through Thursday, 11 a.m.–10 p.m.
Friday and Saturday, 11 a.m.–11 p.m.
Sunday, 4 p.m.–9 p.m.
(636) 946-2468
600 S Fifth St.
www.concettas-stcharles.com

THE CORNER BAR

The building that houses the Corner Bar started out as a military school, training young men even before the Civil War. When the school closed, the building was converted and became the Washington House Hotel. Today it houses the only cocked hat bowling alley in the region and perhaps in the United States. Cocked hat bowling is a three-pin game, and there are two alleys in the basement available for rental as well as play. Upstairs there is a friendly, corner bar that serves daily lunch and a Friday evening meal.

(636) 724-9608
571 First Capitol Dr.

CORNERSTONE CAFE

Cornerstone Cafe serves up freshly made salads, soups, appetizers, sandwiches, burgers, and yummy desserts in a family-friendly environment where soothing yet upbeat Christian music plays in the background. With five flavors of St. Louis's Fitz's root beer on tap, soft-serve Flavor Burst ice cream (up to 4 flavors a swirl), concretes, shakes, and more, kids and adults alike will love Cornerstone Cafe. Located next to the sand volleyball courts, where outdoor seating is also available. Call for carryout.

3245 Rue Royale
www.cornerstonecafestcharles.com

THE CROSSING

Complete with twinkling lights, a fountain, and fire pits, the Wine & Beer Garden at the Crossing is cozy, quaint, and the perfect place to take in some live music. The menu is bistro style with desserts made daily, and guests can dine inside as well.

Wednesday through Friday,
5 p.m.–11 p.m.
Saturday, noon–11 p.m.
Sunday, noon–9 p.m.
(636) 206-5125
3331 Rue Royale
www.thecrossingatnewtown.com

CREATIV EATS

A student-run restaurant at the International Culinary School of the Art Institute of St. Louis, Creativ Eats features a three-course, prix fixe lunch menu on Wednesdays and Thursdays from 11:30 a.m. to 1:30 p.m. when school is in session. At $12 per person, the theme changes monthly and has included Florida-Caribbean fusion, Spanish, Greek, Mexican, and even the "St. Louis World's Fare" in the past. The food is gourmet, but attire is casual. Reservations can be made on Facebook or by calling.

(636) 688-3055
1520 S Fifth St., on the second floor
Find Creativ Eats on Facebook

THE CROOKED TREE COFFEE HOUSE

The Crooked Tree Coffee House was fondly named for the well-known crooked tree at the corner of Kingshighway and First Capitol Drive on the Lindenwood University campus. According to legend, the catalpa tree bows in sadness over the kind Native American chief who was buried below it. Frequented by the college crowd, regular locals, and visitors too, Crooked Tree is the perfect spot for discussing business, studying, or just playing a friendly board game over a cup of coffee. Local musicians are welcome to entertain on the 1824 upright grand piano that's been in the owner's family for nearly 50 years. There isn't a bad seat in the house, as every nook and cranny is cozy. The back patio provides seating for 20 and is perfect for pleasant days and for those who like to have their furry best friend in tow. A full breakfast menu is offered all day, and lunch, tea, and smoothies are also available seven days a week. While there is parking on the right side of the building, it is limited and can be a bit tight maneuvering in and out of the small parking lot. Parking around back is recommended and can be accessed behind the Corner Bar from 6th Street (customers should use the steps by the Corner Bar). Benton and 6th Streets also provide street parking. Go to the website for a list of menu items and current specials. Crooked Tree offers delivery within five miles, and catering is also available.

(636) 669-5282
559 First Capitol Dr.
www.crookedtreecoffee.com

LA CARRETA
With over 75 brands of tequila, it's worth a visit to La Carreta for the drinks alone. The menu goes on forever, with unique appetizers like the La Carreta Dip (a spinach and artichoke jalapeño cheese blend), crab cakes with a Mexican twist, and the roasted corn and tomato soup, which is a meal in itself. There's no shortage of Mexican favorites either, including numerous seafood and steak options. La Carreta offers guests a lively atmosphere to partake in authentic Mexican food.

(636) 922-7775
4203 S Old Hwy. 94

LADY DI'S DINER
Nestled amidst a neighborhood in the heart of St. Charles, Lady Di's is family owned and quite popular with the locals for breakfast and lunch. Don't let the inexpensive menu prices fool you. Generous portions

of traditional (all made with local produce when available) and mouthwatering favorites (like the hash browns made with fresh potatoes) are served up with a smile. Décor is minimal and lends to its small-town charm. Small dogs are allowed on the patio, which is favored seating by many. Call for information about catering.

Monday through Friday,
5 a.m.–1:30 p.m.
Saturday and Sunday, 7 a.m.–1:30 p.m.
(636) 916-4442
630 N Kingshighway St.
www.ladydisdiner.com

MASSA'S

Longtime St. Louis favorite Massa's now offers delicious Italian dishes and fine wine in an upscale atmosphere in St. Charles. Open for lunch and dinner, the spacious patio is also a nice option and is dog friendly. Regulars praise the bartenders for friendly service and the bar gets lively in the evenings with acoustic entertainment and DJs, in addition to karaoke, sports, and ladies' nights. To view the menu (including gluten-free choices) and a list of party pan portions to go (which serve up to 20), visit the website. A second St. Charles County location is in O'Fallon.

(636) 925-2961
3761 New Town Blvd., St. Charles
(636) 561-5202
3072 WingHaven Blvd., O'Fallon
www.stlmassas.com

MISS AIMEE B'S TEA ROOM AND GALLERY

Located in the historic Marten/Becker House built in 1865, Miss Aimee B's harkens back to a time when beauty and charm prevailed. The tearoom serves breakfast and lunch and is available for rental for special events. The Upstairs Shops offer the work of local artists and crafters. Miss Aimee B's also hosts special ticketed events such as lunch with Mark Twain and mystery dinners and luncheons.

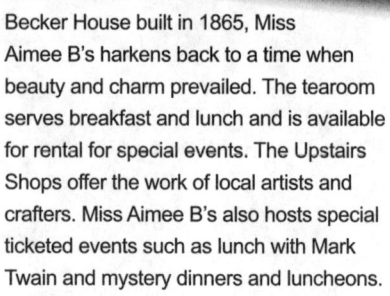

Tuesday through Saturday, 9 a.m.–3 p.m.
Sunday, noon–3 p.m.
(636) 946-4202
837 First Capitol Dr.
www.missaimeeb.com

PIO'S RESTAURANT AND COCKTAIL LOUNGE

Pio's Restaurant and Cocktail Lounge is a family-owned business that has been at its current location since 1954. The building dates back to 1895, when it was a dry goods store with the owner living above. Businesses moved in and out until Pio and his brother-in-law took over half of the first floor and opened a restaurant serving Italian food based on family recipes. The restaurant was successful and expanded to include the entire first floor, then into banquet service.

(636) 724-5919
(636) 946-2522
403 First Capitol Dr.
www.piosrestaurant.com

PRASINO

Voted 2013 Restaurant of the Year by *St. Louis Magazine*, Prasino is a favorite newcomer to St. Charles. Prasino believes in all things green, hence the name, which actually means "green" in Greek. The interior is a blend of modern design and warmth, with much of the wood obtained from old barns. American contemporary plates are concocted with the highest quality of farm-to-table ingredients and are purchased locally whenever possible. Unarguably some of the best in all of St. Louis, the sushi is a popular choice, along with the Paris Benedict (voted Best New Breakfast by *St. Louis Magazine*), the small plate Lobster Avocado, and the Austin Texas (breakfast eggs with chorizo gravy over jalapeño biscuits). Even the more typical menu items such as the flat breads and burgers boast a unique flair. Gluten-free and vegan items are offered as well. Craft cocktails (think ingredients such at St. Germain and cocoa-infused tequila), along with artisanal wines and beer, are available from the bar. When weather permits, the large doors between the patio and bar stand open, allowing the two to meld into one another. These areas are first come, first served, and are quite popular for seating. Private rooms are available for parties or group events. Open daily for breakfast (until 3 p.m.), lunch, and dinner, Prasino is a unique dining experience that should not be missed when visiting St. Charles County. Reservations can be made online or by calling.

(636) 277-0202
1520 S Fifth St.
www.prasino.com

SPIRO'S RESTAURANT

Specializing in classic and remastered Mediterranean dishes, along with their Greek family signature recipes, Spiro's philosophy is that the best food is meant to be shared. Some favorite menu items are the Pepperloin a la Tenderloin, which is hand cut upon each order, the Grecian shrimp, and the saganaki (cheese dipped in beer batter and fried over a large flame right at the table). There's an entrée to please every palate, with several styles of pastas (of course), seafood choices, steaks, and a bevy of desserts. One can't go wrong with the baklava, a Greek favorite. Good wine and attentive service complete the meal. The patio is lovely after dark, when trees with white lights lend to a romantic ambiance. Spiro's also serves lunch at the Foundry Arts Centre on Main Street from 11 a.m. to 2 p.m. on Thursdays. For hours of operation, catering, menu items, and to make reservations for lunch at the Foundry Art Centre, visit the website. Opa!

(636) 916-1454
2275 Bluestone Dr.
www.spiros-restaurant.com

SUGARFIRE SMOKE HOUSE

For the best BBQ around, try Sugarfire Smoke House, where unique dishes like the smoked portobello sandwich, salmon, and fried artichokes stand out on the menu. Traditional meats such as ribs, chicken, brisket, and pork are available, as well as sausage and turkey. Their quality burgers are made from grass-fed beef and are excellent with a fried egg, bacon, or one of the many other add-on options. Their sandwiches, sides, soups, salads, and desserts (including adult-only shakes) are tasty too. Sauces are made in-house and range from sweet to spicy and everything in between (think coffee BBQ sauce). Guests can order authentic BBQ style inside, call for carryout, or drive up and get your order curbside, all where you'll be greeted by the super-friendly staff. Sugarfire caters and has a second St. Charles County location in O'Fallon.

Open daily from 11 a.m. until the food sells out
(636) 724-7601
3150 Elm Point Industrial Dr.
www.sugarfiresmokehouse.com

THE TAP RESTAURANT & BREWERY

As one of the first venues in the state of Missouri to feature a table-top self-pour system, the Tap is popular for this no-wait option and for their selection of more than 300 craft and domestic beers. One hundred percent unfiltered and served directly from the brewing tanks, the Tap's beer is made from only the finest American hops. The restaurant offers a full menu, and the lounge area gets hoppin' after 9 p.m. with a VIP area and full bottle service available. In addition, guests can enjoy a VIP Brew Room experience.

(636) 724-4242
3803 Elm St.
www.gotothetap.com

TUBBY'S PUB 'n GRUB

A favorite among locals, Tubby's is the perfect place to catch the big game or gather with friends for drinks and a savory meal. Charbroiled steaks are their specialty, Tubby's Famous Chicken Nachos are a must-order starter, and the pizza and burgers are super popular too. In addition, they offer tasty menu items such as sandwiches, soup, salad, fish, and homemade desserts. Tubby's is attached to Plaza Lanes (plazalanesbowlingcenter.com) for those who want to bowl. The restaurant caters and has a banquet facility that accommodates up to 130 people. Tubby's is open for lunch and dinner.

(636) 925-1033
506 Droste Rd.

TUCANOS BRAZILIAN GRILL

While pricey, visiting Tucanos is an experience that every meat lover should indulge in at least once. Churrasco (a Portuguese and Spanish word for grilled meat) entrée selections include beef, pork, and poultry prepared in numerous ways and brought to the table on large rotisserie skewers where waiters slice off individual portions onto your plate. There's a seafood selection, grilled vegetables, and pineapple (Yum!) too. The salad bar features a variety of salads, soup, pasta, shrimp, and even quail eggs. In addition, specialty skewers and appetizers are available to order separately. For pricing (kids 6 and under are free with a paying adult while those 7–12 years receive a discounted price), specials, and to receive a free birthday meal, visit the website.

Monday through Saturday, open at 11 a.m.
Closed Sunday
(636) 724-4499
Next to Prasino at 1520 S Fifth St., #100
www.tucanos.com

kids

PLACES TO STAY

EMBASSY SUITES ST. LOUIS—ST. CHARLES HOTEL & SPA

Inviting two-room suites complete with a refrigerator, microwave, and Internet access provide all the conveniences and comfort of home. Separate bedroom and living areas offer more privacy and space. A free cooked-to-order breakfast is available and guests can take advantage of the complimentary evening reception. The Cyprus Grille is perfect for on-site dining, while Caffeina's Marketplace carries Starbucks coffee, gifts, necessities, and snacks. There's an indoor pool, fitness center, and a spa where guests can unwind. Spa Botanica, a rejuvenating and relaxing retreat for adults, also caters to the younger generation. With treatment options designed specifically for them, like the teen facial and Princess Mani/Pedi, they will feel welcome here too. Attached to the St. Charles Convention Center, the Embassy Suites is a convenient choice when doing business or for a relaxing getaway. It is minutes from Lambert Airport as well as St. Charles favorites on Main Street.

(636) 946-5544
2 Convention Center Plz.
www.embassysuites.hilton.com

kids

HAMPTON INN

Offering guests a free hot breakfast and use of an indoor pool, fitness center, and a 24-hour business center, the Hampton Inn is conveniently located off I-70. Extremely accommodating and friendly, the staff has even been known to remove snow from travelers' cars after a heavy snowstorm. Reserve your room online.

(636) 947-6800
3720 West Clay St.
www.hamptoninn3.hilton.com

ENTERTAINMENT/ THINGS TO DO

THE FAMILY ARENA
An ideal option for affordable family entertainment, this venue showcases concerts, MMA boxing, community events, the St. Louis Ambush soccer and Attack football teams, and more. Suites and special event space rentals are available for groups. Visit the website for the event schedule and to learn how to obtain tickets.

(636) 896-4200
2002 Arena Pkwy.
www.familyarena.com

kids

FAST LANE CLASSIC CARS
Rev up your engine and speed on over to Fast Lane Classic Cars, where lookers can spend a good one to two hours oohing and aahing over street rods, Thunderbirds, and countless other eye-catching hot rods. Whether you're in the market for a new car that's old, just want to take a walk down memory lane, or need service on your current classic model, Fast Lane is the place! In business for 20 years, they have a trustworthy and reliable reputation. The fun gift shop carries automotive art, clothing, collectibles, and antiques, which make for great souvenirs. There's even an event space that accommodates up to 100 people and overlooks the main show room, perfect for a party or group event. Visit on Memorial Day for the annual Cobblestone Nationals, a car show attended by thousands. There's judging, music, food, and tons of fun for the whole family.

(636) 940-9969
427 Little Hills Industrial Blvd.
www.fastlanecars.com

kids

81

GLENMARK FARMS

Walkways surrounded by flowers, a background of fields, and a romantic pergola add to the charm of this old-style farm. A farmers market is open here on Saturdays and Sundays, but shoppers can also find their goods at markets around the county, including Lake St. Louis and St. Charles. The simply decorated yet naturally beautiful grounds give the property a romantic feel and make it ideal for a wedding or special event. For additional information or to schedule your event, call or visit the website.

(636) 255-FARM
3516 Shire Ln. in New Town
www.glenmarkfarms.com

LINDENWOOD UNIVERSITY

Lindenwood College was founded in 1827 as a girls' school by Major George Sibley and his wife, Mary. The girls studied in log cabins! A much different picture of Lindenwood University emerges today with its modern buildings and a diverse population of 17,000 students pursuing more than 200 degree programs. The school is still nestled in the grove of linden trees that gave it its name. The university offers many activities such as a speakers series, plays, and musical performances that are open to the public.

(636) 949-2000
209 S Kingshighway
www.lindenwood.edu

PARKVIEW GARDENS

In addition to being the best place in town to purchase fresh floral arrangements, all your garden needs, herbs, and more, Parkview Gardens hosts educational greenhouse tours for kids, book signings, fundraisers, and local community events too. For the current calendar of events, visit the website.

Monday through Friday,
8:30 a.m.–5:30 p.m.
Saturday, 9 a.m.–3 p.m.
(636) 946-7641
(800) 724-1925
1925 Randolph St.
www.parkviewgardens.com

`kids`

ST. CHARLES CITY-COUNTY LIBRARY DISTRICT

The St. Charles City-County Library District is one of the three largest public library systems in the state of Missouri in terms of use. There are 12 branches —three regional branches, four general purpose, two express, and three mini-branches. The regional branches specialize in an area of interest and have larger collections. Kathryn Linnemann Library hosts the Local History and Genealogy collection; Middendorf-Kredell Library houses the Consumer Health collection and is the Federal Documents Depository; and Spencer Library is home to the in-depth collection covering Nonprofit and Business and Public Management. The four general-purpose branches have general interest collections and offer reference services. The two express branches have smaller offerings focusing on popular materials and no reference service. The three mini-branches serve smaller communities with general interest collections.

On almost any day and at any time, the library is hosting a program at one or another site. These include story times, classes, book discussions, author events, and many special programs for all ages. The events are free, although sign-up is recommended.

(636) 441-2300
Multiple locations
www.youranswerplace.org

THE ST. CHARLES CONVENTION CENTER
Playing host to countless events throughout the year, from weddings to the ever popular Home Show, the St. Charles Convention Center is conveniently attached to the Embassy Suites St. Charles Hotel & Spa and is located just off I-70. For information about their services and a calendar of events, go to their website.

(636) 669-3000
1 Convention Center Plz.
www.stcharlesconventioncenter.com

WEHRENBERG ST. CHARLES STADIUM 18 CINE

In addition to regular stadium seating, this movie theater now offers suite seats (for all ages), which include heated seats, couples seating, a food tray, cup holder, electric foot rests, and loads of leg room. Those 21 and older can view movies in the Five Star Lounge from plush, heated leather recliners with food and cocktail table-side service. For movie times and discounted rates, check the website. The Family Summer Series (10 films for $1 each on Wednesday and Thursday during June, July, and August) is a particularly good deal.

(636) 946-1862
1830 S 1st Capitol Dr.
www.wehrenberg.com

kids

TRAVELER'S TIP:

For a hands-on activity, contact the local county hardware and craft stores to enroll in DIY classes and project making. Home Depot (workshops.homedepot.com) offers FREE classes for both adults and kids. Michaels offers classes for adults or lets your child create his or her own project while you shop (classes.michaels.com) and even hosts craft birthday parties. Lowe's offers instructional courses for kids (lowes.com/buildandgrow). Register for most classes online, where you'll find a full description and pricing. Great for a scorching hot summer day or during an unexpected rain shower!

PARKS/TRAILS

With 22 parks in the city of St. Charles, there is no shortage of outdoor space to engage in a friendly game, hike a trail with your pup, swim, play, or, just sit and enjoy what nature has to offer. Below are some of the city's most frequented parks and their popular features. For an inclusive list of the city's parks in addition to what they offer, and specific rules and regulations, visit www.stcharlesparks.com.

BLANCHETTE PARK

Acquired in 1914, this was the city's first park. An abundance of activities are possible, including tennis, swimming, baseball, hiking, biking, and much more. Kids' camps are often held here and there is also a large playground and banquet facility. Two unique features include the Ben Rau Memorial Garden and the Angel of Hope. The latter is a symbol of hope for all parents who have lost a child. A special ceremony takes place here each year on the evening of December 6. The Rau Garden is home to over 50 species of plants; it is quite picturesque when in season. With new weekly blooms, the setting is ever changing and a popular place for pictures and weddings.

1900 West Randolph

FOUNTAIN LAKES PARK

Divided into a north and south side, this park offers annually stocked fishing lakes, paved trails, and natural areas where visitors can view wildlife. In addition, this park is home to a skate park facility, which is coveted by kids. A map detailing features of each side of the park can be downloaded on the park's website.

3850 Huster Road (for skate park)

kids

JEAN BAPTISTE POINT DUSABLE PARK

Often referred to as DuSable Park, it encompasses four different areas. Blanchette Landing has a boat ramp launch area, gazebo, and restrooms, and is a great place to jump on the Katy Trail. The French August Regot Area is just north of Blanchette Landing and has a playground, picnic shelter, and basketball court. Ed Bales Park is a much larger area and includes a playground, three picnic shelters, a ball diamond, a nature area, a hiking and bike trail, and restrooms. In addition, the regularly utilized dog park is located here. With no fee and large separate fenced areas for big and small dogs, it draws visitors from all over the county. Lastly, the Eco Park is an ecological educational area featuring river outlooks, rock and gravel hiking and biking paths, sand trails, and natural areas, as well as a gazebo, which is a lovely place for photos.

MCNAIR PARK

A unique feature of this city park is the Braille Trail. This well-utilized park is divided into two separate areas, with one part used for day camp. With its beautiful plants and flowers, the Botanical Trail is a popular path for walkers. In addition, there is a cross-country course, aquatic center, sand volleyball courts, fields, and many other activities to enjoy.

3050 Droste Rd.

ST. CHARLES HERITAGE MUSEUM AND PARK

The St. Charles Heritage Museum is located in the Cribbin-Kuhlmann House at a site known for many years as Kuhlmann's Grove. The home is beautifully restored and has a number of exhibit rooms in the house itself and in an attached barnlike building. The exhibits cover a range of St. Charles history, focusing on transportation at present. However, the exhibits will change periodically. The displays on the Katy Railroad, American Car and Foundry, and the History of Speed and Travel feature artifacts, information, and interactive touch screens and activities. For example, in the History of Speed and Travel exhibit, visitors may pilot a steamboat down the river (via a screen).

The museum is part of Heritage Park, the trailhead for the Centennial Trail. A two-mile asphalt trail links the museum to the Katy Trail and is part of the regional River Ring, connecting cities throughout the bi-state region. Admission is free, but donations are welcome, and the museum is available for field trips for groups year-round.

Wednesday through Saturday,
10 a.m.–5 p.m.
Sunday, noon–5 p.m.
(636) 949-7535
1630 Heritage Landing, St. Charles
www.stccparks.org

WAPELHORST PARK

While this park has much to offer including a small fishing lake, ball fields, sand courts, and hiking trails, the aquatic center is by far its favorite feature. With swooping slides and play areas for younger kids, it's the perfect family activity for a warm summer day. Experience it for yourself!

1875 Muegge Rd.

kids

WEBSTER/HEATHERBROOK PARK

The newest addition to the St. Charles Parks System is Webster Park. It's unique in that it offers rolling hills, a creek, wooded areas, wetlands, scenic views, and natural settings. There is also a community building here. The trail system connects Webster Park to Heatherbrook Park, which features a fishing lake, large open space, and trails.

100 Wildwood Ct.

WE ALL SCREAM FOR ICE CREAM

DETERS FROZEN CUSTARD

It all started when Deters Dairy was founded way back in 1892 by John J. Deters, a European immigrant from Germany. As the years went by, Deters began bottling, started a Holstein dairy herd, and opened the first Deters Dairy Malt Shop in Quincy, Illinois, in 1948. Grandsons Rich and Greg opened Deters Frozen Custard (a premium French-style ice cream) in 2001, honoring the family tradition. All the typical creamy treats are available, in addition to fruit smoothies, Fitz's Premium Root Beer, Kaldi's coffee, and numerous other delectable menu items. At the Weldon Spring location, you can even get a Chicago-style hot dog made with quality Vienna Beef. Deters takes great pride in making fresh, all-natural custard products, in addition to creating their very own chocolate recipe. For hours, a list of menu items, and the complete history of Deters Frozen Custard, visit the website.

(636) 925-1065
755 Friedens Rd.
(636) 329-8184
804 O'Fallon Rd., Weldon Spring
www.detersfrozencustard.com

DOOZLE'S

Doozle's offers a huge selection of frozen treats like sundaes, malts, ice cream cakes, concretes made with pie, and even frozen dog treats! They sell a lite version of frozen custard too, which is 98 percent fat-free. Find coupons on the web or surprise your guests and invite Doozle's to your party.

(636) 940-0081
3156 Elm Point Industrial Dr., adjacent to Sugarfire Smoke House
www.doozlesfrozencustard.com

LYONS FROZEN CUSTARD

A St. Charles original, Lyons Frozen Custard is popular for meeting friends over a concrete, float, sundae, or other frozen treat. They have a drive-thru too. You'll recognize it by the gazebo out front and kitschy animal décor on the side of the building.

Open seasonally
(636) 925-1448
2309 Elm St.
Find Lyons Frozen Custard on Facebook

SMOOTHIE KING

The original inventor of the smoothie bar and the founder of Smoothie King began blending real fruit with nutrients and protein to improve health and fight food allergies way back in 1973. Since 1989, Smoothie King has been named the No. 1 franchise in their category 20 times by *Entrepreneur* magazine and it's easy to see why. It's a teenager's dream and the perfect adult meal replacement or snack too. With Chobani Greek Yogurt smoothies, enhancers like muscle builders and protein, immune boosters, and supplements, to name just a very few options available, every customer will find the perfect combination. Whether you want to slim down, bulk up, or just delight in a sweet treat, visit Smoothie King seven days a week.

(636) 724-5464
920 S Fifth St.
www.smoothieking.com

U-SWIRL FROZEN YOGURT

With up to 20 nonfat flavors and over 60 toppings, including fresh fruit, U-Swirl Frozen Yogurt offers healthier options in a welcoming environment, encouraging guests to stay awhile. Nutritional facts for each flavor can be found on their website. In addition to yogurt, there's a case of Rocky Mountain Chocolate to appease the sweet tooth of chocolate lovers. They even host parties.

(636) 757-3356
1520 S Fifth St., Ste. 105
www.u-swirl.com

YO MY GOODNESS

With only 100 calories and zero grams of fat, this is one creamy cool snack you can justify eating. Fill up at the self-serve dispensers and head to the counter where countless toppings await. Choose your favorites to create the perfect concoction to please your palate. Nutrition facts can be found on the website.

(636) 922-1245
2621 Muegge Rd.
www.yomystl.com

KIDS

BOSCHERTOWN GRAND PRIX

For good times and fast go-karts, head to Boschertown Grand Prix, where they have been "fueling the need for speed" since 1957. Riders can maneuver S-curves, banked turns, and long straightaways in standard go-karts (10 years and up), sprint-karts (16 years and up), and super-karts (18 years and up). Double seaters are available for younger kids to ride along. Call for special party rates. Hours are seasonal and dictated by the weather; however, the track often remains open when it rains.

(636) 946-4848
3500 N Hwy. 94 (1.4 miles north of Hwy. 370)
www.boschertowngokarts.com

DEMOLITION BALL/ADRENALINE ZONE

The Adrenaline Zone is one of the largest multilevel laser tag arenas in the state. At 8,000 square feet, it accommodates up to three teams at 10 players each. Players must be 7 years of age or older. Guests may also want to attempt "the Heist" (newly renovated), a state-of-the-art timed laser maze that can be rented by play or by the hour. Demolition Ball combines the games of hockey, polo, football, and basketball and is played in bumper cars. The object is to shoot a Wiffle ball through a circular goal with a handheld scoop. Players must be 54" tall and at least 12 years old. In addition, there are video games, pool tables, foosball, and concessions. Walk-ins are accepted, but reservations are recommended. Visit the website for rates and party rental information. (Catering is available through Filas Market Catering.)

Open daily at noon
(636) 940-7700
1875 Old Hwy. 94 S
www.db-az.com

DIERBERGS SCHOOL OF COOKING

An array of courses are offered in the class kitchen for kids and are fun for parties, to take with a few friends, or as a grandparent or parent/child activity. Visit the website and click on the Culinary Classes & Events tab to choose a class and register online or call for more information.

(636) 669-0049
2021 Zumbehl Rd.
www.dierbergs.com/school

THE PAINTED POT

Kids and adults can create their own ceramic, glass, pottery, and mosaic art pieces. Walk-ins are welcome, but guests can also attend special events like Margarita Madness or Story Time Fun, hold parties, or take a class here. All the products are nontoxic, lead free, water based and washable, as well as dishwasher-, food-, and microwave-safe. Visit the website for rates and to print coupons.

Closed Mondays
(636) 300-4515
3772 Monticello Plz.
www.thepaintedpotstl.com

PUMP IT UP

With oversized inflatables for all ages, this is the perfect place to burn off some energy when the weather isn't cooperating for outdoor activities. Socks are required and jumpers must be at least 34″ tall. All guests must sign a waiver and those under 17 years old need to have a parent or guardian signature. In addition to open jump times, Pump It Up offers private party rental and special events like Jump-n-Jam or Parents' Night Out. Be sure to check the calendar for availability, scheduled open and event jumps, and coupons. Supervision is provided and the inflatables are wiped down regularly.

(636) 946-9663
3691 New Town Blvd.
www.pumpitupparty.com/st-charles-mo

SKATEBOARD PARK

With three interconnected deep bowls, a streetscape, obstacles, and rails, both fun and challenges await for skaters of all skill levels at this 13,000-square-foot park. Skate boarders are welcome every day, but parents should know that the park is unsupervised. For rules and regulations along with a map of the park layout, go to the city park website and click on the Facilities tab.

Daily, 10 a.m.–dusk
3740 Huster Rd.
www.stcharlesparks.com

SWING-A-ROUND

Featuring an 18-hole miniature golf course, softball and baseball batting cages, an arcade, and concessions, Swing-A-Round is a great place to spend a few hours with friends or family. Visitors are recommended to call for party reservations and specific hours.

Open daily, April through October, weather permitting
(636) 947-4487
3541 Veterans Memorial Pkwy. (visible from I-70)
www.swing-a-round.com

ST. CHARLES NEIGHBORHOODS - WEST

ST. PETERS

Originally founded by French traders in the late 18th century, a large influx of German immigrants settled here from 1830 to 1850. St. Peters has a population of approximately 53,000 people today and *Money* magazine put the city on its list of Top 100 Best Places to Live in the country in 2008, 2010, and 2012. In 1999, it became the first city in St. Charles County to become a part of Tree City USA, sponsored by the National Arbor Day Foundation. The program recognizes municipalities that demonstrate a strong commitment to responsible urban forestry management, and applicants must reapply each year. Since 2000, St. Peters has earned four consecutive Tree City USA Growth Awards in recognition of ongoing efforts to improve its program. Only a fraction of the Tree City USA communities earn these awards each year. The city has 25 beautiful parks, a strong arts culture, a large variety of entertainment, numerous shopping opportunities, and tons of activities offered through the Rec-Plex, all of which are great draws for both residents and visitors alike.

SHOPPING

BARNES & NOBLE

In addition to reading materials, this large retailer carries music, toys, and gifts and also has an in-store cafe where shoppers can purchase Starbucks products. Storytelling, reading, and other events take place in the children's section, while authors frequent the store for signings. The store opens daily at 9 a.m.

(636) 278-1118
320 Mid Rivers Ctr.
www.barnesandnoble.com

CALISA HOME DÉCOR

Specializing in upscale resale furniture and home décor, Calisa offers high-end pieces that shoppers won't find elsewhere at discounted prices. While stock is ever changing, you can view some of their current merchandise on their website. The shop offers delivery for larger items.

Closed Monday and Tuesday
(636) 970-0069
3354 Mid Rivers Mall Dr.
www.calisahomedecor.com

DESIGNER RESALE BOUTIQUE

Designer Resale Boutique carries ladies merchandise and is open daily, with consignment items accepted Monday through Wednesday and on Sundays. Merchandise ranges from quality jeans, handbags, jewelry, and shoes to furs and formal wear, as well as everything in between. Items are only on the floor for 60 days and are discounted after 30.

Monday through Friday, 10 a.m.–6 p.m.
Saturday, 10 a.m.–5 p.m.
Sunday, noon–4 p.m.
(636) 279-3968
344 Mid Rivers Mall Dr.
www.drboutique.com

MID RIVERS MALL

Mid Rivers Mall offers more than 100 retailers, including anchors Dillard's, Macy's, Dick's Sporting Goods, JC Penney, and Sears. The Wehrenberg Mid Rivers 14 Cine is also here and show tickets can be purchased directly through Fandango on the mall website, which also provides a list of stores, a directory map, hours, and current retailer coupons.

1600 Mid Rivers Mall Dr.
www.shopmidriversmall.com

MY SON'S CAKE & CANDY SUPPLY

A one-stop shop for all your bakery supplies, this store carries everything from tools to toppings. The knowledgeable staff is on hand to answer questions for the novice baker, but it also has an extensive product line for professionals to choose from. In addition, it offers decorating classes that include cupcake decorating, figure piping, and more.

(636) 279-3729
117 Main St.
www.stlouiscakeandcandysupplies.com

TREATS UNLEASHED

Once pups catch a whiff of the homemade organic treats and a glimpse of the large selection of toys, tails start a-waggin'! Treats Unleashed stocks all the latest dog and cat essentials, including stylish collars and leashes, interactive toys, all types of food, grooming aids, and much more. You can drop Fido off to be bathed or do it yourself at their self-washing station, schedule a pet portrait, or attend a class on current pet topics such as dental health or raw diets. Treats Unleashed even makes cakes for all occasions. Be sure to bring your furry friend along to help sniff out all the great deals and to get a free treat. Visit the website for the shop's dog blog and events calendar.

(636) 970-7730
306 Mid Rivers Ctr.
www.treats-unleashed.com

VALENTI'S MARKET & CATERING CO.

For a quick and tasty sandwich, Italian and American fare, bakery items including pie, fresh produce, wine, sauces, and more, head to Valenti's Market & Catering. In business since 1937, Valenti's offers quality meats as well as ingredients for making dinner at home. Their homemade house dressing is delicious and the staff is helpful and friendly. Packages and catering are available too.

(636) 970-2992
6750 Mexico Rd.
www.valentismarket.com

THE WHITE HARE

Offering elegant and stylish home décor, custom florals, and unique gifts with an emphasis on customer service, the White Hare was opened in 2003 by a mother-daughter team. Since then, they have doubled in size and moved to their current location. With furniture, accessories, boutique clothing, and more filling the 7,300-square-foot space, shoppers could spend hours just browsing, but are sure to leave with more than they intended to buy. Classes are also available, as well as a popular in-home accessory service. Classes, held at 7 p.m., are a reasonable $10 each and are nonrefundable. Attendees must register within the store.

(636) 441-1111
6121 Mid Rivers Mall Dr.
www.thewhitehare.com

RESTAURANTS/DINING

CALECO'S

In business for 36 years, Caleco's takes pride in being a true St. Louis original. The extensive menu offers steaks, pastas, seafood, pizza, sandwiches, salads, and much more. Kids will be endlessly entertained by the saltwater aquarium and by the train that runs over the bar. With tons of TVs, guests can enjoy Italian cuisine and never miss a play, but the best place to dine is the enchanting patio, which is surrounded by live greenery and snaking plant vines decorated with white lights.

(636) 970-7926
269 Salt Lick Rd.
www.calecos.com

kids

CRAZY SUSHI

In addition to scrumptious sushi, a large variety of fish, beef, pork, and chicken dishes are offered here along with soups, salads, appetizers, and desserts. BBQ beef ribs, pork dumplings, sautéed scallops, and chicken teriyaki are just a few of the many choices. Open for lunch and dinner, Crazy Sushi closes in between the two meals and on Sundays. For hours, visit the website.

(636) 397-2414
3350 Mid Rivers Mall Dr.
www.crazysushimo.com

ELMER'S TAVERN

Elmer's just celebrated its 100th birthday in 2014, and this historic local hangout is filled with nostalgia, old photos, and other interesting memorabilia that will keep your eyes glued to the walls while you're sipping a cold one. Regulars enjoy watching our much-loved St. Louis Cardinals and other local sports teams, playing billiards, and just catching up with familiar faces at this favorite watering hole. TJ's Pizza is available, but you're better off having a few beers and heading down the block to Hobo's for some of the best catfish and fried chicken around.

(636) 397-9592
8 Main St.

FIRST WATCH

Voted "Favorite Daily Breakfast, Favorite Brunch, Favorite Diner" by *Sauce Magazine*, First Watch has a customer-first policy and offers healthier options that are still delicious. They leave the whole pot of coffee at your table and have freshly squeezed orange juice. Catchy entrée names like the Chickichanga, Bacado Omelet, and Not Guilty Your Honor, along with the finest and freshest of ingredients, make it difficult to choose. Diners can substitute healthier solutions or special order their food just the way they like it. Kids will love it here too, with a menu just for them. Breakfast, brunch, and lunch items are all available from 7 a.m. to 2:30 p.m. Nutritional facts and a gluten-free guide are available on the website.

Open daily, 7:00 a.m.–2:30 p.m.
(636) 970-0050
312 Mid Rivers Ctr.
www.firstwatch.com

HOBOS

Located inside the American Legion, this full-service restaurant isn't just for members. Menu favorites include fried chicken, catfish, ribs, and pulled pork. They pride themselves on keeping things simple, yet they smoke everything on-site and use their own blend of seasonings and spices for the rub. Visit the website for a list of daily specials or call to order carryout. Hobo's also caters.

(636) 278-2828
200 Main St.
www.hobocooker.com

JOE'S CRAB SHACK

A seafood lover's paradise, Joe's offers a huge variety of fish prepared any and every which way you can imagine. For those less enamored by the sea, the Cheesy Chicken and the burger are tasty too. The Crab Nachos make for a great start while the Crab Cake Caesar Salad is a nice twist on regular ole greens. The Grilled Malibu Shrimp and Samuel Adams Steampot are stellar choices, along with the fresh catch Redfish 'N Lobster dish.

Open daily at 11 a.m.
(636) 397-0733
5856 Suemandy Dr.
(Visible from I-70, but it requires a little meandering to get to.)
www.joescrabshack.com

MAIN STREET DINER

While at first glance you might think you're in the wrong place, you'll be pleasantly surprised when you're greeted with a smile and the homey décor upon walking through the door. Large portions of delicious, down-home, cooked-to-order breakfasts and lunches can be enjoyed inside or on the large covered patio out back. The menu goes on and on, with a kids' section, a list of favorites like the reuben, and daily specials too, such as the country-fried steak. Adult beverages including beer, wine, and mixed drinks are available as well. Main Street Diner can be rented out for private parties and also caters personal and corporate events. This is one place you'll leave full and satisfied! For daily specials and a complete list of menu items, visit the website.

Tuesday through Saturday, 6 a.m.–2 p.m.
Sunday, 6 a.m.–1 p.m. (breakfast only)
Closed Monday
(636) 397-6260
315 Main St. in Old Towne
www.mainstreetdiner.org

MARIO'S DONUTS & CAFE

With an extensive menu of breakfast items, vegetarian options, and American and Mediterranean choices, every customer's craving will be satisfied here. Aside from the donuts, which are baked fresh daily, there's a Southwest burrito, breakfast sandwiches, omelets, and more for morning time. Lunch and dinner choices range from Greek salads, gyros, and chicken sandwiches to hot dogs, burgers, and fries. Baklava and other sinfully sweet pastries and desserts are on display to tempt your taste buds too. Some healthier and trendier options include the baba ghanoush, falafel, and hummus. Coffees of all kinds, soft drinks, and fruit smoothies round out the menu.

Monday through Friday, 5:30 a.m.–8 p.m.
Saturday, 6 a.m.–8 p.m.
Sunday, 6 a.m.–4 p.m.
(636) 447-4515
2786 Muegge Rd.
www.cafemario.com

kids

PIRRONE'S PIZZA
Don't let the name fool you. With numerous other fish and Italian options, Pirrone's is more than just a pizza joint. However, the freshly made-to-order pizza is a popular choice. Guests can enjoy local game time and daily happy hour specials, as well as an affordable lunch buffet Monday through Friday from 11 a.m. to 2 p.m.

(636) 278-3800
299 Salt Lick Rd.
www.pirronespizza.com

SHAMROCKS PUB n GRILL
Order up some Irish fare like the Guinness Lamb Stew or Bangers 'n' Mash, throw some darts, or challenge friends to some bag games. Traditional menu items like burgers (the Top 'O Da Mornin is succulent!), signature pizzas, salads, and sandwiches are offered too, and guests can build their own Pot O' Gold by combining their favorite appetizers. Beer drinkers will appreciate the 20 rotating flavors on tap and music lovers can enjoy live entertainment on Friday and Saturday nights. For the calendar of events and to view the full menu, visit the website. Pets are always welcome on the patio.

(636) 939-2000
4177 Veterans Memorial Pkwy.
www.shamrocks-pubandgrill.com

SNIBO'S SPORTS BAR
Serving up everything from steaks (watch for specials), seafood, chicken, and pizza to healthy salads and low-carb menu options, Snibo's makes all of their dishes from scratch. It's the perfect place to relax with a drink on the patio, engage in a friendly game of washers, darts, shuffleboard, or pool, or to watch the big game on TV. Snibo's delivers, caters, and even offers call-ahead ordering so your food is ready and waiting at your table when you arrive.

Open seven days a week for lunch and dinner
Monday through Friday, 10:30 a.m.–1:30 a.m.
Saturday, 11:30 a.m.–1:30 a.m.
Sunday, noon–midnight
(636) 441-4496
2129 Parkway Dr.
www.snibos.com

PLACES TO STAY

DRURY INN ST. PETERS

Whether you're traveling for business or pleasure, the Drury Inn is a great value! Tastefully appointed rooms, as well as two-room suites, provide guests with all the essentials, including refrigerators, microwaves, and free wireless Internet. The Free Quikstart hot breakfast includes eggs, sausage, biscuits and gravy, waffles, and more while the Free Kickback (from 5:30 p.m. to 7 p.m.) is more than enough for dinner. Kid favorites like chicken strips, mac and cheese, meatballs with pasta, and hot dogs are just some of the options on the rotating menu, in addition to soup, salad, and baked potatoes. As an afternoon snack, guests can help themselves to popcorn and soda. There's an indoor pool, whirlpool, and 24-hour business and fitness centers. The Drury is also super pet-friendly, requiring only a $10 cleaning fee with a signed waiver. Located just off I-70, the hotel sits adjacent to Mid Rivers Mall next door to Bob Evans.

(636) 397-9700
170 Mid Rivers Mall Cir.
www.druryhotels.com

370 LAKESIDE PARK

With 50 full-service RV sites, as well as both individual and group primitive tent sites, all types of campers will be satisfied. Guests receive special rates for fishing and the boat launch, but they differ based on your site location, so campers will need to inquire with the park about rates and fees. All RV sites have nearby comfort stations, picnic tables on concrete pads, and free Wi-Fi. The roads are paved and there is a convenience store for supplies. Amenities vary between the individual and group tent sites; however, the group sites do not have access to water, sewer, or electric. The park is located off I-370, and additional information can be found on the city's website under the Parks tab.

www.stpetersmo.net

ENTERTAINMENT/THINGS TO DO

> **TRAVELER'S TIP:**
>
> Go to www.stpetersmo.net and choose Leisure Line on the left to view Leisure Line Online. Choose from the extensive list of interests for a guide to the city's recreation, cultural classes, golf, and city events.

BRUNSWICK ZONE XL

Jam-packed with activities for all ages, this is one place where adults will actually have as much fun as kids. Grown-ups will love the Sunday Fun Day Door Buster, which offers breakfast, Bloody Marys, and games for just $5 each. Strikerz Bar & Grill offers adult beverages, but it is also a full-service restaurant where families can dine together while watching their favorite team on big-screen TVs. There's a second bar near the 38 bowling lanes too. Leagues are offered for all ages and skill levels, including a family league, couples bowl, and Club 50+ (for those aged 50 years and older), just to name a few. Trained coaches are available for All-Star Varsity, with a $500 college scholarship awarded to a player in Division II between the ages of 12 and 20 years upon college admission. In addition to bowling, guests can play laser tag, pool, and darts, or visit the giant game room. Visit the website for specials and information about lessons, leagues, and group events (including fundraising and nonprofits, where they'll prepare anything from pasta to prime rib).

(636) 474-2695
8070 Veterans Memorial Pkwy.
www.bowlbrunswick.com

kids

CAVE SPRINGS LANES

With 32 lanes, touch screens, and auto scoring, Cave Springs Lanes is perfect for the novice or avid bowler. Birthday parties and group events are commonplace here, and there's a snack bar providing pizza and other fast-food items. Coupons can be found online.

(636) 441-1774
4055 Mexico Rd.
www.cavespringslanes.com

GREAT SKATE

Roller skating, lessons, and party packages (including Adult Late Night) are available for all ages at this rink. The facility is also where the highly competitive women's roller derby team, St. Chux Derby Chix, practices, in addition to local dance and figure skating clubs. Great Skate is also available for roller hockey, soccer, and dodgeball rental. For regular weekend, school break, and holiday hours, visit the website.

(636) 441-2530
130 Boone Hills Dr.
www.greatskaterocks.com

`kids`

KOKOMO JOE'S FAMILY FUN CENTER

For indoor family fun, visit Kokomo Joe's, where admission is free and you only pay for what you play. Choose from go-karts, bumper cars, mini-bowling, glow-in-the-dark mini-golf, laser tag, the bounce beach, inflatables, and arcade games. Once you've worked up an appetite, hit the Snack Shack for the usual snack items, pizza, wraps, and more. The facility is open daily, but you'll want to check the website for weekday specials. Visit for Toddler Time on Wednesdays or Unlimited Laser Tag on Fridays, or schedule a party or group event. Visit the website for information and coupons.

(636) 447-5656
4105 N Cloverleaf
www.kjfun.com

kids

MID RIVERS 14 CINE
For current shows and movie times, log on to the website or call.
(800) FANDANGO
1220 Mid Rivers Mall Dr.
www.wehrenberg.com

ST. CHARLES COUNTY COMMUNITY COLLEGE
In addition to providing education, the college is a big player when it comes to offering entertainment within the community. The venue has played host to Summer Movie Night, the Food Truck Frolic, speakers, musicals, plays, and other fun outings like the popular Chocolate, Wine, & All That Jazz event.

(636) 922-8469
4601 Mid Rivers Mall Dr.
www.stchas.edu

ST. PETERS CULTURAL ARTS CENTRE
Located at city hall, the Cultural Arts Centre hosts numerous activities here including art exhibits, displays, camps, and classes, in addition to theater and musical performances. The space is also available to rent for private events.

(636) 397-6903
1 St. Peters Centre Blvd.
www.stpetersmo.net

kids

ST. PETERS REC-PLEX

This fitness and sports facility offers a plethora of opportunities for visitors, like the 3,300-square-foot pool, which has a 130-foot waterslide, play features, a vortex, and current channel. Public ice skating sessions, the basketball and volleyball courts, and classes are also popular. In addition, parts of the facility can be rented out for parties. There's also a food court and arcade. To learn about admission, classes, and daily membership fees, and to view a calendar of events, log on to the city's website.

(636) 939-2386
5200 Mexico Rd.
www.stpetersmo.net.

kids

FESTIVALS/EVENTS

CELEBRATE ST. PETERS COMMUNITY FESTIVAL

Held in September, this event has music, food, games, carnival rides, and even fireworks! The celebration takes place by the lake in 370 Lakeside Park off Highway 70 (Exit 2 on Lakeside Drive). Pets, outside alcohol, and coolers are not allowed at this event, but concessions are available for purchase.

370 Lakeside Park
www.stpetersmo.net

kids

OCTOBER HARVEST

In addition to selling beautiful plants and flowers, Daniel's Farm and Greenhouse is loads of fun for kids too. This annual fall event includes a straw maze, a petting zoo, tube slides, a fort maze, and antique farm equipment to play on, in addition to the popular Pony Express Train Ride, to name a few. Stop by to scout out the perfect pumpkin and to enjoy some fall fun.

352 Jungermann Rd.
www.danielsfarmandgreenhouse.com

kids

SUNSET FRIDAYS

Visit the city's website for a schedule of concerts offered on Fridays at 370 Lakeside Park. The musical event is held seasonally on the dock at the marina. Gator Grill Island is open for concertgoers to grab a bite and a beverage to enjoy while listening to local talent.

370 Lakeside Park
www.stpetersmo.net

PARKS/TRAILS

For information about all of the parks in St. Peters and the features of each, log on to www.stpetersmo.net.

370 LAKESIDE PARK

At 300 acres, 370 Lakeside Park is the largest of the St. Peters parks. The 140-acre recreational lake offers fishing and boating with electric trolling motors. There are biking and pedestrian trails, an RV park, and primitive tent campsites. Leashed pets are welcome. Canoes, kayaks, paddle boats, bikes, and jon boats are available to rent. Future plans include a playground, sand volleyball, an archery range, and a dog park with a water feature. Seasonal concerts take place on some Fridays at the marina on the dock (check the city's website for dates). Gator Island Grill is open to purchase food during concerts.

370 Lakeside Park

CITY CENTRE

Located adjacent to the St. Peters Rec-Plex and city hall, this park offers an abundance of activities. There are free concerts and movies at the outdoor amphitheater, pavilions with BBQ grills, a playground, trails, and fields for baseball, soccer, and football. The gazebo is great for photo taking and is also popular for weddings. A Veterans Memorial, honoring all branches of the military, is also located here.

1 St. Peters Centre Blvd.

LAUREL PARK
While mainly used by residents, this 40-acre park offers guests lots of fun too. Features of the park include two lakes, roller hockey, pavilions, a trail, volleyball courts, horseshoe pits, a pool, ball fields, and a playground.

181 Driftwood Ln.

OLD TOWNE PARK
At more than 100 years old, this was St. Peters's first park and remains a favorite of residents today. In addition to ball fields, pavilions, horseshoe pits, and a playground, a two-story log cabin that was originally built around 1835 sits across the street. The homestead was reconstructed in 2004 and now hosts annual visits and photos with Santa.

1 Park St.
(at Park Street and North Gatty Drive)

ST. PETERS GOLF & RECREATION CENTER
This park features an 18-hole municipal golf course, a banquet hall, tennis courts, and a 13-acre fishing lake, as well as an outdoor swimming pool.

200 Salt Lick Rd. (Quick access to the course can also be gained from Dardenne Park at 175 Dew Court.)

WE ALL SCREAM FOR ICE CREAM

FRITZ'S FROZEN CUSTARD
Made with fresh natural ingredients and an "old time" freezing process, Fritz's is tops when it comes to custard. With the original 90 percent fat-free vanilla, the lite 95 percent fat-free vanilla, and a no-sugar-added vanilla available, even diabetics and those counting calories can indulge. The rich, full-bodied chocolate is always an option too, in addition to the flavor of the day. Order up your favorite custard treat or purchase some to take home. You can visit Fritz's in O'Fallon and Wentzville too. For a list of menu items and the Flavor of the Day calendar, as well as seasonal hours, log on to the website.

(636) 928-2606
506 Jungermann Rd.
www.fritzsfrozencustard.com

OBERWEIS DAIRY
Providing quality products since 1951, Oberweis offers ice cream, pies, cakes, drinkable yogurt, fountain treats, and other yummy desserts. In addition, the store has a grocery section with dairy products such as cheese, butter, and yogurt, as well as farm fresh eggs, bacon, fruit juices and more. A unique service provided to customers is the ice cream treat delivery, which is perfect for a small group, large party, or event. A $15 minimum order is required along with a delivery charge of $2.75. A large portion of the dairy's success is due to the fact that its products contain quality ingredients and are rBGH-free. Oberweis also offers a long list of products that are gluten-free and kosher. This information, along with a kids club and nutritional facts, can be found on their website.

(630) 897-6600
7090 Mexico Rd.
www.oberweis.com

kids

ORANGE LEAF

With flavors ranging from the classic tart to popular picks like cookies and cream, in addition to unexpected creations like the key lime pie, there truly is a flavor to please everyone. They even have holiday choices like pumpkin pie and egg nog latte. Smoothies, no-sugar, and dairy-free options are available too. Orange Leaf is quite proud of their "cool spoons," which feature an aerodynamic handle and shovel shape and can be used for more than feeding your mouth. Visit the website to view fun spoon creations or to submit your own. Fill up your cup with some self-serve and choose your pile-on toppings. Orange Leaf yogurt is also available in O'Fallon.

(636) 278-2605
308 Mid Rivers Mall Dr.
www.orangeleafyogurt.com

SILKY'S FROZEN CUSTARD

For sundaes, concretes, shakes, malts, and more made with super-smooth ice cream, visit Silky's. They offer countless flavors and toppings, with real whipped cream, chocolate syrup, and free sprinkles. Quarts to go are available along with lighter choices too.

(636) 477-1444
3885 Mid Rivers Mall Dr.
www.silkyfreeze.com

ST. CHARLES NEIGHBORHOODS – WEST

COTTLEVILLE

One of the oldest towns in St. Charles County, Cottleville was settled by Captain Warren Cottle just before 1800 and was home to Camp Krekel, a famous recruiting camp during the Civil War. Today, Missouri State Road N, which runs through Cottleville, is a much different sight than when it was an Indian trail, Boone's Lick Road, and the Western Plank Road. Unfortunately, the plank road made from timber began to warp and rot away not long after it was constructed in the 1850s. This path connecting St. Charles to Cottleville saw covered wagons; Daniel Boone's sons, who used it to reach a salt lick; cattle being driven to auctions and to the railroad; troops transporting supplies during the Civil War; and pony express riders; among others. It was once a principal highway that led westward through Missouri, and it was often used to branch off to the Oregon, California, and Santa Fe Trails. Spanish grant settlers also used it as a route between St. Charles City and their farms. Today, Cottleville is a destination town within the county, and although it's small, it lures visitors and locals alike who want to experience one-of-a-kind restaurants and unique places of business.

SHOPPING

ALY'S INTERIORS

For unique and high-quality gift items, home décor, accessories, and clothing, you must visit Aly's. This designer boutique offers the newest and trendiest clothing from the Dallas, Los Angeles, Las Vegas, and Chicago markets, in addition to jewelry, handbags, St. Louis Cardinals apparel, floral arrangements, artwork, furniture, and more. Aly's skilled designers are available to assist you in the store using their full library or in your home where they can help with window treatments, paint colors, furniture placement, artwork, and accessorizing. To view recently added merchandise and place orders online, log on to the website.

Monday through Saturday, 10 a.m.–5 p.m.
Thursdays, 10 a.m.–7 p.m.
October through December—Open Sunday from noon to 4 p.m. to accommodate shoppers' holiday needs.
(636) 939-2597
5359 Hwy. N, Ste. 202
alysinteriors.com

THE BLACK SHEEP

Specializing in monogramming, this cute boutique is the perfect stop for purchasing gift items. They can be found on Facebook.

Opens at 10 a.m., Tuesday through Saturday
(636) 939-9366
5359 Hwy. N

MANNINO'S MARKET

Passed down through four generations, Mannino's is tops for all your meat, produce, and deli needs. Their quality meats are hand-cut daily and they use their own family recipe for the freshly made Italian sausage. Lunch specials, Italian cheeses, homemade spiedini, spices, and bakery items can be purchased here as well as seasonal items like firewood, Christmas trees, and fresh turkeys for the holidays.

Open daily at 8 a.m.
(636) 441-7755
5205 Hwy. N North
www.manninosmarket.com

RESTAURANTS/DINING

BEMO'S

The staff at Bemo's wants you to eat, drink, and enjoy! Cozy up to the bar near the stone fireplace on a cool day, dine on the patio as you watch passersby, or order one of their signature entrées in the indoor dining room. In addition to numerous signature dishes (like braised pot roast), Bemo's offers guests a wide variety of appetizers, pastas, sandwiches, burgers, salads, and soups to choose from along with a separate kids menu. Visit on Thursday nights for live music. A private area for banquets or group rentals for 10 to 50 guests is also available. Call for reservations.

(636) 939-9922
5373 Hwy. N
www.bemosgrill.com

COTTLEVILLE WINE SELLER

With over 3,000 bottles of fermented libations from more than 200 labels around the world, it's easy to see why this is a wine lovers paradise. However, with fire pits, soothing waterfalls, and a heated pavilion, the property itself is a giant outdoor oasis for anyone wanting to relax with a drink, share a meal with friends and family, or take in some live entertainment. Appetizers, salads, wraps, and more are available, but the menu is limited on Friday and Saturday evenings, as well as some Sundays. The small original building on the property houses gift items and dates way back to 1849, where it was constructed right on Plank Rd. A beautiful location for group gatherings, this establishment is a popular place for weddings. Weather permitting, the Cottleville Wine Seller opens daily at noon, but has seasonal hours. View the event calendar on the website.

(636) 244-4453
5314 Hwy. N
www.cottlevillewineseller.com

EXIT 6 BREWERY

As the first nanobrewery (a scaled-down microbrewery) in St. Charles County, Exit 6 appeals to a wide range of palates. With around 70 craft beers and an ever changing tap list, as well as bottled beer, there's something to please everyone. Their biggest seller is the Vanilla Cream Ale, but some prefer the Smoked Blond Pilsner (described as drinking a pilsner while eating bacon by a campfire), or the ever popular Pumpkin. There is no smoking and no kitchen, but guests are welcome to bring their own snacks or order delivery (Exit 6 provides the menus) to eat inside or on the patio. For beer lovers who want a unique experience, visit Exit 6 Brewery. Opens daily at 4 p.m.

(636) 244-4343
5055 Hwy. N, Ste. 113
www.exit6brewery.com

PLANK ROAD PIZZA

One of the oldest buildings in Cottleville houses Plank Road Pizza, named after the Western Plank Road that connected St. Charles to Cottleville in 1851. Much of the accent woodwork and indoor booths are made from the original attic floor or wood from local barns. Priding themselves on "keeping it local," Plank Road Pizza features beer from local breweries such as Schlafly and Four Hands, as well as tea and coffee from the locally owned Thomas Coffee. All the contractors used to restore the building call the St. Charles area home. The restaurant's sauce and dough are made fresh daily for gourmet pizzas ranging from traditional and specialty, to brunch and dessert. Even the kids menu is interesting; it includes a PB&J version of pizza made with their original crust. They also feature a monthly special. In addition to the cozy indoor eating area, there are two quaint, yet spacious outdoor patio areas. Plank Road Pizza does not have a phone number, but takeout orders may be placed online.

5212 Hwy. N
www.plankroadpizza.com

THE RACK HOUSE WEST WINERY

The newly opened Rack House West Winery serves its own blends, in addition to West Winery Wines. The premium whiskey and bourbon lists are quite impressive, while microbrew beer is also available. Menu items include bar bites, small plates, salads, paninis, flatbreads, and dessert. The large back patio is quite pleasant and accommodates furry friends too. Unique features of the winery include the ventilated cigar lounge located right inside the winery and glass windows showcasing barrels for winemaking. A large back room is available for private parties (call for requirements and reservations). For special events, visit the website.

Open daily at 11 a.m.
(636) 244-0574
5065 N Hwy. N
www.rackhouse.westwinery.com

SE7EN CUPCAKES AND MARTINIS

Specializing in sweet sins and sinful sweets, Se7en Cupcakes and Martinis offers both cupcakes and martinis in seven delightful flavors. Choose from Lust (red velvet), Gluttony (salted caramel pretzel), Greed (carrot cake), Sloth (lemon), Wrath (chocolate/vanilla), Envy (strawberry), Pride (birthday cake), or one of the special monthly flavors. Guests can also order wine (from Cupcake Vineyards, of course), drinks with top-shelf liquors, and appetizers. Cigars (from Aiello's across the street) are available for purchase here and can be enjoyed on the patio, where well-behaved dogs are welcome too. Gluten-free cupcakes are available every Tuesday and Thursday. Sinful hour is from 3 p.m. to 6 p.m., Monday through Thursday, but you can indulge in sweet sins every day of the week. Visit the website to see menu items and like them on Facebook for daily specials.

(636) 244-5185
5045 N Hwy. N
www.se7encupcakesandmartinis.com

STONE SOUP COTTAGE

An intimate and sought-after dining experience, Stone Soup Cottage has received countless awards and is one of St. Charles County's absolute gems. Reservations are required and recommended weeks to months in advance. The prix fixe six-course menu for parties of eight or less changes every four weeks and is determined by availability of the current season's locally produced ingredients. Guests are invited to take in the sweeping views and explore the property before and after dinner. At $90 per plate, without drinks or tip included, it's pricey, but the experience is truly unique and offers guests a taste of something delectable and different. Wine flights are offered with the meal for an additional fee, but guests may bring their own. A corkage fee of $35 does apply, with a limit of two bottles. Diners should also note the hefty cancellation fee, which is necessary due to the high demand for seating. Dress is typically business casual. The cooking classes are less expensive (at $65 per person) and are also quite popular. In addition, Stone Soup Cottage hosts wild game dinners and private events. The Stone Soup Cottage Cookbook is available for purchase for those who want to try preparing some of the chef's creations at home, with 20 percent of sales going to the local Boys & Girls Clubs of St. Charles County. To view the current menu and to learn more about Stone Soup Cottage, go to the website. Please call for reservations.

(636) 244-2233
5809 Hwy. N
www.stonesoupcottage.com

ENTERTAINMENT/THINGS TO DO

AIELLO'S CIGAR BAR

Sit back and relax on the patio with a cigar, play some bocce ball or watch the big game here. Their covered and heated patios are also available for group rental. The annual Taste of Italy is held here and features Italian food vendors, a band, and bocce ball, and Texas Hold 'Em tournaments that benefit charity.

Open daily
(636) 441-0994
5286 Hwy. N
www.aielloscigarbar.com

ST. PAT'S DAY PARADE AND RUN FOR THE HELMET

More than 65,000 participants filled the streets of Cottleville in 2014 for this annual super-fun event. Proceeds from the parade go to the St. Pat's Foundation, which benefits the local community. Runners and walkers can register online for the Fire Fighters' Run for the Helmet and receive a race T-shirt. For parade entry information, to register for the run, or to see a route and map of the festivities, log on to the website.

www.stpatparade.org

PARKS/TRAILS

LEGACY PARK
The city council named the park, hoping that the "legacy" of growing for tomorrow will always continue for Cottleville. Park features include playgrounds, shelters, tennis courts, basketball goals, a multi-use trail, a multipurpose amphitheater, and the Bark Park. The popular one-acre fenced dog park is well maintained and has both a large dog and small dog side. The Panting for Paws 5k and 1 mile walk are held here. In addition, park goers can enjoy live music, haunted hayrides, and food trucks. Legacy Park is conveniently accessible to Vantage Park at the pedestrian bridge. Future plans include numerous fields for a variety of sports and additional shelters.

www.cityofcottleville.com

VANTAGE PARK
Named for Vantage Homes, which donated 23 acres of land for the park, it draws fishermen with its nine-acre stocked lake and the annual Fishing Derby in the spring. The catch and release rule is in effect here. With multiple trails that connect directly to the one that surrounds the lake, opportunities to encounter wildlife are frequent. In addition, the Dardenne Greenway Trail connects to the park via a 10-foot-wide pedestrian bridge that leads to Legacy Park.

www.cityofcottleville.com

ST. CHARLES NEIGHBORHOODS – NORTHWEST

O'FALLON

While there is no written history of the area prior to 1673, it is believed that Native Americans lived in what is present-day O'Fallon possibly as early as 800 BC. The area provided fertile ground where they trapped, fished, and hunted. Originally a trail established by animals, the Salt River Road was traveled by Native Americans who collected salt from the evaporated Salt River. Nonnative residence isn't noted until 1796, when Jacob Zumwalt and his brothers settled here in order to create better lives for their families. His fort was the largest of its kind in the county at that time, and due to its central location and stability, it was used for protection by numerous families who sought shelter during the War of 1812. During the years from 1856 to 1870, the settlement saw much growth. It was named for John O'Fallon, a business man, noted soldier, and public-minded philanthropist. Historical features like Zumwalt's Fort, named for the early pioneers who helped establish and grow the city, pepper the area.

RESTAURANTS/DINING

BLUE SKY CAFE & BAR

Whether you're a "Crazy Redhead," a "Classy Girl," or you just need an "Attitude Adjustment," Blue Sky is right up your alley if martinis are your drink of choice! If you're up for a challenge, join the martini club by drinking 52 different flavors of the 60 offered (all with fun names like the three mentioned above) and get your name on a plaque on the wall. Before you know it, you'll be feeling like a "Mellow Russian" saying "It's French to Me" and doing the "Midnight Tango." Order the martini of the week and get a discount. Be sure to fill that tummy with one of Blue Sky's tasty appetizers, sandwiches, or entrées (the homemade chips are a must). If martinis aren't your thing, you can choose from one of the many beers (including three Missouri and five craft beers, along with import and domestic), wines, or cocktails on the beverage list. Bring your pup and enjoy the shaded patio.

(636) 561-6919
9999 WingHaven Blvd.
www.blueskystl.com

BRISTOL SEAFOOD GRILL

For fine fresh seafood and succulent steaks, dine at Bristol for lunch, brunch, or dinner. In addition to the many fish options, there are delicious sides, desserts, and countless wine choices. The restaurant offers a large gluten-free menu, as well as vegetarian choices, and even includes a craft beer. The half-off Sunday wine special allows guests to purchase half-price bottles up to $100, and 25 percent off those $100 and up. For a $15 welcome offer, a free birthday entrée, and more, join their e-mail list by logging on to the website. Bristol Seafood Grill is an excellent choice for seafood lovers!

(636) 625-6350
2314 Technology Dr.
www.bristolseafoodgrill.com

CAPP'S RESTAURANT

Also known as Cappuccino's, Capp's started out as a coffeehouse, but now serves breakfast and lunch menu items all day, as well as dinner. Generous portions of home-style, made-from-scratch favorites made with fresh, local ingredients make this restaurant a standout. Down-home dishes like the chicken and dumplings are popular, but the breakfast burrito is their top seller. Also available to cater or for private events, you'll find additional information and the Cardinal Special, which is offered during all home and away games at the website.

(636) 980-2326
1365 Hwy. K
www.cappuccinosrestaurant.net

ETHYL'S SMOKEHOUSE & SALOON

Delicious smoked BBQ in a fun yet relaxed environment makes Ethyl's a huge hit. With sand volleyball courts, a new outdoor sandbar with 17 TVs, and a playground, it's an ideal place for families to unwind together. Some favorites include the world-famous Hot Chickie Stripper, Queso Kettle Chips, and Pig in the Garden, but guests love the catfish, burgers, and sides too. Kids eat free on Mondays with the purchase of an adult entrée. There's Imperial Dancing on Tuesdays, a DJ on Fridays and Saturdays, and live music the last Saturday of each month. The building itself dates back to 1926 and has been a drinking and eating establishment ever since. Look for the old gas pumps out front and sand courts in the back. Visit the website for daily lunch specials, soups of the week, special events, or to join Ethyl's Club and receive $5 off.

Open daily at 11 a.m.
(636) 978-7755
8505 Veterans Memorial Pkwy.
www.ethylssmokehouse.com

kids

HEAVEN SCENT BAKERY

The solution for anyone needing a sugar fix day or night, Heaven Scent Bakery is open from 4 a.m. to 9 p.m. every day except Christmas and has a 24-hour drive-thru! Choose from a huge selection of lip-licking pastries, in addition to donuts, chocolate-covered strawberries, ice cream treats, cannoli, and even gourmet pies. With numerous awards over the years, this bakery is quite popular for their wedding cakes, but offers all-occasion and photo cakes too. For a heavenly day, be sure to stop by!

Open daily except Christmas, 4 a.m.–9 p.m.
Drive-thru open 24 hours a day
(636) 240-8311
1133 Bryan Rd.
www.heavenscentbakery.com

JJ TWIG'S PIZZA & PUB

Home of the drool-worthy Original Double Decker (yep, that's double crust, double meat, and double cheese), JJ Twig's uses 55-year-old recipes for sauce, pizza dough, and Italian sausage, in addition to 100 percent whole milk mozzarella. Aside from the popular Double Decker, guests can order thin-crust pizza, appetizers, sandwiches, pasta, and salads. They even make their own cole slaw.

(636) 379-4446
1090 Tom Ginnever Ave.
www.jjtwigsstl.com

KITARO BISTRO OF JAPAN

This upscale restaurant with contemporary décor offers more than just a meal. Serving steak, seafood, and sushi, in addition to specialty entrées, KiTARO offers guests a unique experience as they watch their food being prepared in front of them. KiTARO is also available for private parties.

(636) 300-4422
4551 State Hwy. K
www.kitarojapan.com

MASSA'S

For great Italian cuisine, visit this longtime favorite. While the inside is nice, the patio is where it's at. With both covered and uncovered areas, guests can dine lakeside by the fountain on a sunny day, sit under the twinkling lights with a glass of wine at night, or stay dry and cool on a rainy day while watching a game on TV. For musical entertainment visit Massa's on Thursday night.

(636) 561-5202
3072 WingHaven Blvd.
www.stlmassas.com

MCGURK'S PUBLIC HOUSE

Serving up traditional pub food along with Irish favorites, McGurk's is warm and inviting with its large wooden bar and lively atmosphere. However, seating on the garden-like patio, complete with a fountain and waterfall, is coveted. Go where the locals go for fish and chips, a tall mug full of Guinness, Irish whiskey, and tasty pub grub.

(636) 978-9640
108 S Main St.
www.mcgurkspublichouse.com

PANTERA'S PIZZA

Mouthwatering pizza, a long list of appetizers, sandwiches, and salads make this family-friendly restaurant the perfect choice. With a game room, big-screen TV, and free drink refills, Pantera's is ideal for a kids' party or team celebration. Dine in or carry out seven days. Guests can even order a half-bake and finish cooking it at home to enjoy fresh, warm pizza right out of the oven. For hours, party reservations, and fundraiser information, log on to the website.

(636) 272-7600
22 O'Fallon Square
www.panterasofallon.com

kids

PIGGY'S BAR BQ

Touting numerous awards, including Best BBQ by *Rural Missouri* magazine from 2008 to 2014, Piggy's offers Kansas City–style BBQ to eat in or carry out, and it caters too. The Full Slab Friday special is popular, and diners can find coupons online at the website. Travelers heading east on I-70 towards O'Fallon will surely notice the "Hot Tasty Butts" billboard, advertising the restaurant's best asset.

(636) 272-7444
327 S Main St.
www.piggysbarbq.com

RENDEZVOUS CAFE & WINE BAR

An absolute gem, the Rendezvous Cafe & Wine Bar offers elegant dining, wine tastings, classes, live music, and other special events. Sip one of 400 different wines, which can be purchased by the flight, glass, or bottle, with glass and flight flavors changing at the beginning of each month. A full bar with liquors, adult coffee drinks and 25 ever changing microbrews are available as well. All-day breakfast, tapas, pizza, and gourmet coffee and teas lure guests back. A popular spot for large parties, the establishment has a lovely outdoor patio and wine and banquet rooms. Take a cooking class, paint your own wine glass, or attend a Murder Mystery Dinner, all while savoring your favorite wine.

(636) 281-2233
217 S Main St.
www.rendezvouscafeandwinebar.com

SEÑORA ESPINOS TAQUERIA

Boasting fresh Mexican with unique style, guests are in for a treat when ordering customer faves like the Burrito Bandito or Espinos Nachos. The menu offers something for everyone, including vegetarian choices, a kids' list, and breakfast on Saturday and Sunday. While the décor inside is charming, the outdoor patio is super cute, too, and well-behaved furry friends are welcome.

Open seven days a week
(636) 272-9001
840 Bryan Rd.
www.espinosmexicanbargrill.com

STEFANINA'S PIZZERIA & RESTAURANT
This O'Fallon location was the first Stefanina's to open back in 1981 and customers keep coming back for Stef's original Sicilian pasta, steak, chicken, and pizza recipes. For a peek at the menu of this much-loved establishment or to find other locations in the county, visit the website.

(636) 272-3499
8645 Veterans Memorial Pkwy.
www.stefspizza.com
Visit www.saveatable.com/stefspizza to book a table online and receive a discount.

SUGARFIRE SMOKE HOUSE
Unique flavors like the smoked portobello sandwich, salmon, and fried artichokes make Sugarfire a standout! Traditional meats such as ribs, chicken, brisket, and pork are available, as well as sausage and turkey. Their quality burgers are made from grass-fed beef and are excellent with a fried egg, bacon, or one of the many other add-on options. Their sandwiches, sides, soups, salads, and desserts (including adult-only shakes) are tasty too. Sauces are made in-house and range from sweet to spicy and everything in between (think coffee BBQ sauce). Sugarfire offers catering and has a second St. Charles County location at 3150 Elm Point Industrial Drive in St. Charles.

Open daily from 11 a.m. until the food sells out.
(636) 265-1234
9955 WingHaven Blvd.
www.sugarfiresmokehouse.com

WE ALL SCREAM FOR ICE CREAM

BASKIN ROBBINS

The Baskin Robbins 31-flavor concept was developed in 1953 to create a flavor for each day of the month. This longtime favorite is still pleasing customers daily. They offer individual cones, sundaes, blasts, smoothies, and shakes, as well as ice cream cakes, pies, and other sweet treats. This location has a convenient drive-thru.

(636) 379-2039
512 S Main St.
www.baskinrobbins.com

CARNIVAL FROZEN CUSTARD

In addition to yummy frozen custard, countless flavors of shaved ice, smoothies, sundaes, and other cold goodies, they offer supreme funnel cakes topped with fruit and ice cream.

Hours are seasonal.
(636) 281-2653
114 Triad Ctr.
Find Carnival Frozen Custard on Facebook

FRITZ'S FROZEN CUSTARD

Made with fresh natural ingredients and an "old time" freezing process, Fritz's is tops when it comes to custard. With the original 90 percent fat-free vanilla, the lite 95 percent fat-free vanilla, and a no-sugar-added vanilla available, even diabetics and those counting calories can indulge. The rich, full-bodied chocolate is always an option too, in addition to the flavor of the day. Order up your favorite custard treat or purchase some to take home. You can visit Fritz's in Wentzville and St. Peters too. For a list of menu items and the Flavor of the Day calendar, as well as hours that change seasonally, log on to the website.

(636) 379-2799
2453 Hwy. K
www.fritzsfrozencustard.com

JO-JO'Z FROZEN YOGURT

Offering innovative flavors on the healthy side, Jo-Jo'z has 14 premium flavors, nonfat yogurt, sugar-free yogurt, dairy- and lactose-free sorbet, custard, and over 40 toppings to choose from. With choices like Mangosunrise, Irish Mint, Pomegranate Raspberry, and good old-fashioned Country Vanilla, you won't be able to resist. Jo-Jo'z is available for parties and offers business and bulk delivery. For nutritional information, a list of current flavors, and savings, visit the website.

(636) 439-1599
3449 Pheasant Meadows Dr., Ste. 105
www.jojozfroyo.com

ORANGE LEAF FROZEN YOGURT

With flavors ranging from the classic tart to popular picks like cookies and cream, in addition to unexpected creations like the key lime pie, there truly is a flavor to please everyone. They even have holiday choices like pumpkin pie and egg nog latte. Smoothies, no-sugar, and dairy-free options are available too. Orange Leaf is quite proud of their "cool spoons," which feature an aerodynamic handle and shovel shape and can be used for more than feeding your mouth. Visit the website to view fun spoon creations or to submit your own. Fill up your cup with some self-serve and choose your pile-on toppings. Orange Leaf frozen yogurt is also available in St. Peters.

(636) 272-6006
349 Winding Woods Ctr.
www.orangeleafyogurt.com

SMOOTHIE KING

The original inventor of the smoothie bar and the founder of Smoothie King began blending real fruit with nutrients and protein to improve health and fight food allergies way back in 1973. Since 1989, Smoothie King has been named the No. 1 franchise in their category 20 times by *Entrepreneur* magazine, and it's easy to see why. It's a teenager's dream and the perfect adult meal replacement or snack, too. With Chobani Greek Yogurt smoothies, enhancers like muscle builders and protein, immune boosters, and supplements, to name just a very few options available, every customer will find the perfect combination. Whether you want to slim down, bulk up, or just delight in a sweet treat, visit Smoothie King.

Open seven days a week
(636) 294-7849
1314 State Hwy. K
www.smoothieking.com

O'FALLON/DARDENNE PRAIRIE

SHOPPING

BELLA BRIDE
Bella Bride touts exceptional value for high-quality bridal merchandise and attentive personal service.

Monday through Thursday, 11 a.m.–7 p.m.
Friday and Saturday, 10 a.m.–4 p.m.
Sunday (January through April),
noon–4 p.m.
(636) 625-1330
3028 WingHaven Blvd., O'Fallon
www.bellabrideshop.com

C. RALLO MEAT COMPANY
An Italian Marketplace, C. Rallo's has been in business since 1901 and is now run by its third generation of Rallo sons. Selling only USDA choice Black Angus beef, all-natural chicken and pork products, sandwiches, homemade salads, and other grocery items, it's an ideal place to get everything you need for a barbecue in one of O'Fallon's beautiful parks. They carry Boar's Head products, which are gluten-free, and their hamburger is ground fresh daily. In addition to offering an assortment of meat packages (including half-hogs), they process deer and wild game.

Open seven days a week
(636) 474-1300
1302 Sunburst Dr., O'Fallon
www.crallomeatmarket.com

DESIGNERS BOUTIQUE & GIFTS
Opened by three moms, Designers Boutique & Gifts carries unique jewelry, accessories, and home décor, much of which is created by local designers. Shoppers have the option to personalize their items through monogramming and other artistic touches. In addition, the shop offers classes, parties, and registries, and it even has a full-service salon in-house. Come prepared to shop—their merchandise is super cute and irresistible!

(636) 625-4474
9987 WingHaven Blvd., O'Fallon
www.shopdesignersboutique.com

MOM'S FAMILY RESALE
For new and gently used clothing, accessories, shoes, furniture, toys, and more.

(636) 272-6667
274 Ft. Zumwalt Square, O'Fallon
www.momsfamilyresale.com

O'FALLON MAIN STREET MARKETPLACE
You'll find a large variety of vintage goods, antiques, collectibles, furniture, and décor at this large market place. In addition, you can learn how to make that old piece of furniture new again by enrolling in one of their painting classes. All supplies are provided so you only need to bring the item you want to transform. For information about classes and to shop online, visit the website.

Tuesday through Friday, 10 a.m.–6 p.m.
Saturday, 10 a.m.–5 p.m.
(636) 272-5735

220 S. Main St., O'Fallon
www.ofallonmainstreetmarketplace.com

SUSIE Q QUILTING
With new fabric arriving each week, other in-stock supplies, and classes, quilters will find all that they need to complete their quilting projects.

(636) 272-7455
1676 Bryan Rd., #106, Dardenne Prairie.
www.susieqquilting.com

TIC-TOC SHOP
In business for 47 years, the Tic-Toc Shop carries the finest brands of grandfather, mantel, and wall clocks and offers a unique shopping experience. In-home repairs are completed by certified servicemen, and delivery is available too.

(636) 240-1033
614 School St., O'Fallon
www.tic-tocclock.com

PLACES TO STAY

HILTON GARDEN INN

The rooms and suites at the Hilton Garden Inn are quite comfortable and are a convenient choice for travelers. The free shuttle transports guests wherever they want to go within a 5-mile radius, and there's a full-service restaurant open for breakfast, lunch, dinner, and evening room service too. In addition, snacks are available 24 hours a day at the Pavilion Pantry. Guests can unwind in the lounge, take a dip in the heated pool and whirlpool, get a workout in at the fitness center, or catch up on work in the 24-hour business center. Packages are available and reservations can be made online.

(636) 625-2700
2310 Technology Dr., O'Fallon
www.hiltongardeninn3.hilton.com

THE RESIDENCE INN

This all-suite hotel features large, modern rooms with separate living spaces, a complimentary social hour, grocery service, exercise room, and a full-service business center. Passes to Gold's gym are available too. Pets are allowed with a $100 nonrefundable cleaning fee, and guests should call the hotel directly for specific information regarding the pet policy.

(636) 300-3535
101 Progress Point Ct., O'Fallon
www.marriott.com

ENTERTAINMENT/THINGS TO DO

9-11 MEMORIAL: A TRIBUTE TO FIRST RESPONDERS
Located at city hall, this 17-foot monument is made from 22 tons of steel from the 9-11 tragedy. It honors 346 firefighters and 37 police officers, all of whom were victims. Inside city hall, visitors can view a piece of the red steel core from the original World Trade Center.

100 North Main St., O'Fallon

DESIGN2BREW
As a fully licensed, on-premise retail wine making and brewing center and supply store, there is a large selection of beer-, wine-, cider-, and mead-making kits, in addition to ingredients, equipment, and books for purchase. Design2Brew also offers hands-on workshops, as well as classes for the beginner to the advanced artisan.

(636) 265-0751
9995 WingHaven Blvd., O'Fallon
www.design2brew.com

JUMP 4 FUN
With indoor inflatables for toddlers and big kids, open play time, and family jump nights, this party and play center will put a smile on any child's face. In addition, Jump 4 Fun will host your party with assistance from staff members and provide cake, ice cream, and soft drinks. Cakes (including large cookies and cupcakes) can be brought in by the guest of honor. All jumpers must provide a signed waiver and staff members always appreciate tips. If you plan on making 10 jump visits, it makes sense to purchase a $42 pass. The website has a helpful FAQ page that answers most common questions. It's always party time at Jump 4 Fun!

(636) 329-1811
79 Hubble Dr., Ste. 103, Dardenne Prairie
www.jump4funstl.com

LILLIAN YAHN GALLERY

The St. Charles County Arts Council offers exhibits, shows, classes, and events at the Lillian Yahn Gallery. For a schedule of events, visit the website.

Closed Sunday and Monday
(636) 561-0028
7443 Village Center Dr. in the WingHaven development, O'Fallon
www.stcharlesart.org

LOG CABIN MUSEUM

Collections of artifacts including a dollhouse-size replica of Zumwalt's Fort, Wabash Railroad items, 19th-century hats and clothing, an immigrant's trunk, a folding bed for covered wagon travel, a Regina talking machine, a portable organ used at weddings and funerals, and 1950s beauty parlor equipment are some of the items available for viewing.

May through September, 2nd and 4th Sundays, noon–3 p.m.
Open for special events and by appointment
(636) 240-2000
308 Civic Park Dr., O'Fallon
www.ofallon.mo.us/log-cabin-museum

OMAR J. DAMES WAR MEMORIAL

One of the first in the nation to honor U.S. soldiers killed in the Vietnam War, this memorial was erected in 1969 in Civic Park. It was dedicated to World War I veteran and Missouri legislator Omar Dames on September 21, 1969, then restored by the city, moved to Dames Park (land that had belonged to the Dames family), and rededicated on Veterans Day in 2003. The names of 17 St. Charles County soldiers who died in Vietnam are listed.

387 Dames Park Dr., O'Fallon
www.ofallon.mo.us/parks&rec/dames-park

OZZIE SMITH SPORTS COMPLEX

This 76-acre park features the T. R. Hughes Ballpark, the St. Charles County Amateur Sports Hall of Fame, seven outdoor baseball/softball diamonds for league play, restrooms, a concession stand, and a playground. The T. R. Hughes Ballpark is home to the River City Rascals minor league baseball team and makes for a fun and very affordable family outing. Visit the team's website for tickets, pricing, and game schedule. With the purchase of a game ticket, admission into the St. Charles County Amateur Sports Hall of Fame is free. MVPs, state champions, and other local athletes who played dartball, football, bowling, horseshoes, baseball, and softball are honored here. On display is a vintage collection of sports memorabilia, trophies, pics, pennants, souvenirs, records, and awards. In addition, the top high school athletes are recognized, along with community members who supported amateur sports in St. Charles County.

(636) 379-5614
900 T. R. Hughes Blvd., O'Fallon
mseymour@ofallon.mo.us
www.ofallon.mo.us.com

PAINTING WITH A TWIST
The new and trendy Painting with a Twist invites you to bring your own wine or beverage and join friends in painting a masterpiece. Offering parties, showers, couples nights, team building, and more for adults as well as kids, Painting with a Twist provides the canvas, paint, and brushes. Guests can find the schedule of events and register for special projects online. Visit Painting with a Twist, where the motto is "a little bit of paint, a little bit of wine, a whole lot of fun."

(636) 625-7928
3004 WingHaven Blvd., O'Fallon
www.paintingwithatwist.com/ofallon

REGAL O'FALLON STADIUM 14
For current movie showings and times, log on to the website listed below or call.

(800) FANDANGO
900 Caledonia Dr., O'Fallon
www.fandango.com

RENAUD SPIRIT CENTER
The Renaud Spirit Center celebrated its 10th anniversary in 2014 and features basketball and volleyball courts, a multipurpose space, and a huge indoor aquatics center. The natatorium features an interactive play structure, lap lanes, a 185-foot slide, a vortex, and a lazy river. The facility is also home to the Cultural Arts Center, where the public can view exhibits and meet the artists. Kids camps, classes, and other events are hosted here as well.

2650 Tri Sports Cir., O'Fallon
www.renaudspiritcenter.com

VETERANS MEMORIAL WALK

With the platoon of cast bronze boots arranged in marching order, flags representing all branches of the service, and the eternal burning flame, the Veterans Memorial Walk is quite moving. The memorial honors all U.S. past and present soldiers, with thousands visiting each year. It is free to view and open to the public all day, year-round. It is available for special occasions with permission.

800 Belleau Creek Rd., O'Fallon

WEHRENBERG TOWN SQUARE 12 CINE

For current showings and times call or log on to the website.

FANDANGO
7805 Hwy. N, Dardenne Prairie
www.wehrenberg.com

FESTIVALS/EVENTS

CABIN FEVER DAZE
This super-kid-friendly event held in January boasts an outdoor skate rink, human dogsled races, food trucks, a kids area, live music, and free activities and entertainment. Visit the website for a full list of events.

www.ofallon.mo.us

kids

CELEBRATION OF LIGHTS
Visitors can experience this holiday event in several different ways. The drive-through version is a great option for frigid nights or for people with small children or pets. Reservations are necessary for train, carriage, and sleigh rides, as well as Segway tours (16 years and up). The Old-Fashioned Holiday Stroll walk-through night is quite popular, but no pets are allowed this night. Caroling, Santa pics, food, fireworks, and vendors complete the festivities. Specific days and times, fees, and discounts can be found on the website. The celebration is held in November and December in Fort Zumwalt Park.

www.ofallon.mo.us

kids 🐾

FALL FEST & STREET DANCE
FREE entertainment and music draw a crowd for this two-day October event. In addition to a street dance on Friday night and the Fall Fest run on Saturday, there's shopping, a variety of vendors, and a scarecrow costume contest. This event is held in Civic Park.

www.ofallon.mo.us

FOOD TRUCK FRENZY
Once a month from June through August, there's a Food Truck Frenzy in Fort Zumwalt Park. Bring a blanket and chairs and get ready to eat and mingle. The dates of the event and a list of food trucks attending are listed on the website. Admission and parking are free.

www.ofallon.mo.us/food-truck-frenzy

HERITAGE & FREEDOM FEST
A kid zone, fireworks, free concerts, the parade, a carnival and games on the midway, food, and vendors make this

two-day Fourth of July celebration a perfect event for the whole family. Parking is free. For the schedule of events, visit the website.

www.heritageandfreedomfest.com

kids

O'FALLON FOUNDERS' DAY

Kids will get a kick out of the free 19th-century, hands-on activities they can experience at Fort Zumwalt Park in May. Some activities include cow milking, washing clothes by hand, stilt walking, watching raw wool being spun into thread, and soap carving. Games, demonstrations, live music, food, vendors, and entertainment round out this celebration.

www.ofallon.mo.us

kids

O'FALLON JAMMIN'

This family-friendly and free outdoor concert series takes place in Civic Park from June through August. Log on to the website for the schedule of events.

www.ofallon.mo.us

TREE LIGHTING CEREMONY

The lighting takes place in the O'Fallon City Hall rotunda and is complemented by live choral music, a visiting Santa, holiday games, crafts, and vendors. Concessions are available for purchase, but there is no charge for admission or the kids' activities.

www.ofallon.mo.us

kids

PARKS/TRAILS

CIVIC PARK

A favorite feature of Civic Park is Alligator's Creek Aquatic Center, which has a lazy river, vortex, springboard, water playground, and twisting water slides. Those using the slides must be at least 48" tall. Promotional days are popular too, with themes like Dive-In Movie Night and the Cardboard Boat Race. Resident, nonresident, daily, and season passes are available for purchase. The park also has a bandstand, two playgrounds (one is ADA-accessible), horseshoe pits, and trails. It is home to the O'Fallon Historical Society Log Cabin Museum, which can be toured by appointment or during special events. The Pool Paws Dog Swim (benefitting the Missouri Alliance for Animal Legislation), O'Fallon Jammin', and the annual Fall Fest and Street Dance also take place here. This park is the oldest in the city.

308 Civic Park Dr., O'Fallon
www.ofallon.mo.us

DARDENNE PRAIRIE CITY HALL PARK

This community park is located behind city hall. With a bandstand for entertainment, the "Spray Ground Play Ground," and concessions available during events, it is a popular place for families to enjoy. The annual Dardenne Prairie Easter Egg Hunt takes place here and the Family Pavilion can be rented too.

2032 Hanley Rd., Dardenne Prairie
www.dardenneprairie.org/parks-rec/

GEORGETOWN PARK

This beautifully landscaped park holds a monument dedicated to fallen soldiers on both sides of the Civil War.

At the corner of Feise and Henke Roads, Dardenne Prairie
www.dardenneprairie.org/parks-rec/

WESTOFF PARK

This park features the Westoff Plaza Skate & BMX Complex and Brendan's Playground. With a custom-built concrete design, the Westoff Plaza Skate and BMX complex features obstacles for all skill levels. Challenges include bank and quarter-pipe ramps, a stair set, hubba ledges, a mini volcano, a jump gap, and a six-foot bowl, in addition to grind rails and ledges. Brendan's Playground is O'Fallon's first all-inclusive playground.

810 Sheppard Dr., O'Fallon
www.ofallon.mo.us

kids

YOUTH ACTIVITY PARK

As the largest outdoor supervised skate park in Missouri, the park boasts 33,000 square feet of skate course for skateboarders, inline skaters, scooters, and BMX bikers (helmets are required). In addition, the park has sand volleyball, indoor rock climbing, a large gaming area, and half-court basketball. Fright Night, open play, and other parties and events take place here, making it a favorite among kids. For requirements and to purchase passes, log on to the website.

7801 State Hwy. N, Dardenne Prairie
www.sccmo.org

kids

FT. ZUMWALT PARK

Located in historic (and scenic) Fort Zumwalt Park in O'Fallon, Zumwalt's Fort dates back to St. Charles County's days as a frontier outpost. Jacob Zumwalt had lived in Kentucky near Daniel Boone. He took advantage of land grants the Spanish government handed out circa 1798, and obtained 300 acres including the area that now comprises Fort Zumwalt Park. The log building was the Zumwalt family's home and also the first meeting place for the Methodist church in St. Charles County when a service was held there in 1807. During the War of 1812, it became a "settler fort," protecting as many as ten frontier families from attack by Native Americans (although there are no recorded attacks, only threats). The center chimney is the only original section of the house remaining. The structure is in the process of being rebuilt by the O'Fallon Community Foundation.

Nearby is the Darius Heald House. Nathan and Rebekah Heald purchased the Zumwalt property in 1817 after surviving the War of 1812. Nathan was commander of Fort Dearborn near Chicago when they came under fire. He was wounded and captured by Native American attackers and his wife, Rebekah, who was also captured, suffered a broken arm and six wounds. When her captors observed her using a riding crop to fend off an attempt to steal her blanket, they were favorably impressed with her spunk and tended her wounds. They later sold her for a mule and a bottle of whiskey. The man who traded for her reunited her with Nathan and after three months and a 1,907-mile journey, they returned home to Louisville, Kentucky. It helped that Rebekah had the foresight to sew money into Nathan's clothing.

The Heald family lived in the original Zumwalt cabin where their son Darius was born. They established the first school in the area in the 1820s. Darius grew up to be a prominent citizen, donating land for a new Methodist church, insuring that there was a school for young women, and serving as a Missouri legislator. He built the brick home in 1884.

This historic home with German-Italianate-Victorian architecture, hipped-roof construction, and coal-burning fireplaces (which have since been converted to gas), was restored in 2001, while maintaining the original interior woodwork and reopening the fireplaces. The property was originally built between 1884 and 1886 on Darius Heald's farm, which he called "Stony Point Plantation."

The Heald Home is available for tours by appointment or during special events. For information call (636) 379-5614.

Fort Zumwalt Park is also the site of the St. Charles County Model Railroad Club. The facility is open to the public to view the railroad layouts on Friday, 7 p.m.–9 p.m., and Saturday and Sunday, 1 p.m.–6 p.m. Donations are welcome.

(636) 379-5606
1000 Jessup Ln., O'Fallon
www.ofallon.mo.us/parks&rec/fort-zumwalt-park

kids

LAKE ST. LOUIS

Conveniently located between Interstates 70 and 64, Lake St. Louis encompasses two lakes, which are the main focus of the city. Now with more than 14,000 residents, Lake St. Louis began as a private recreational lake community in 1966 and then became a city in 1975. Some interesting residents have included Nelly (Cornell Haynes Jr.), the Grammy Award–winning music artist, as well as past NFL St. Louis Cardinals coach Don Coryell and Shaun Murray, a four-time world championship wake boarder. One must be a member of the Lake St. Louis Community Association or a guest of a member to use the lakes, golf course, and tennis courts or to visit the clubhouse pools. However, travelers will be lured in by the city's other notable features, like the National Equestrian Center, local parks, and shopping.

SHOPPING

BOULEVARD BRIDE
Whether you're looking for the perfect wedding, prom, or homecoming dress or gown, you'll want to visit Boulevard Bride. Unique styles and the option to special order assure shoppers they won't find the same designs here as at malls and other local retailers. In addition, Boulevard Bride offers an heirloom redesign service, removing stains and repairing damage to vintage dresses. Their experts will even collaborate with you to create a new look for your gown while maintaining the integrity of the original design. Tux rental and alterations are offered as well. Appointments are preferred for brides and wedding parties.

Tuesday through Thursday, 11 a.m.–7 p.m.
Friday and Saturday, 10 a.m.–4 p.m.
Many Sundays from January to May
(636) 561-4030
300 Lake St. Louis Blvd.
www.boulevardbride.com

LAKE ST. LOUIS FARMERS AND ARTISTS MARKET
As St. Charles County's ONLY producer-only market, shoppers will find a wide variety of goods (approximately 75 vendors!) produced by the vendors themselves. In addition to baked goods, local produce, and art, the market offers kids' activities, live music, yoga, and educational programs in health, art, food, and gardening on select Saturdays. Even local breweries and wineries participate, offering samples to market goers later in the season. Located at the Meadows shopping center. Call the Meadows shopping center or visit the website for more information.

Mid-April through mid-October, Saturdays, 8:00 a.m.–noon
(636) 695-2626
www.lakestlouisfarmersandartistsmarket.com

kids

THE MEADOWS
Offering premier shopping in an open-air style, the Meadows at Lake Saint Louis is located just off I-64/US 40. The only Von Maur department store in Missouri is here, as well as a Nike Factory store, Victoria's Secret, Altar'd State, Chico's, and Francesa Collections, just to name a few. Some of the specialty stores include Sebastien's Pet Salon and Aveda Salon Kashmir. With approximately 40 retailers, there's a store to please every shopper. The mall is home to BC's Kitchen and the Lake St. Louis Farmers and Artists Market.

Monday through Saturday, 10 a.m.–9 p.m.
Sunday, 11 a.m.–6 p.m.
20 Meadows Circle Dr.
www.themeadowsatlsl.com

SHOPPES AT HAWK RIDGE SHOPPING CENTER
Located on the south side of Lake St. Louis at the intersection of Hwy. N and US Hwy. 40, this was the largest retail project in St.Charles County at the time of its development. Anchor stores include Walmart, Lowes, Sports Authority, T.J. Maxx, as well as numerous other retailers.

RESTAURANTS/DINING

BC'S KITCHEN
Serving modern American cuisine, chef and owner Bill Cardwell believes that eating is about more than just good food. He has explored how dining has changed over time and strives to treat guests to a special experience, not just a meal. Boasting fresh local ingredients in creative recipes such as the vegan-friendly vegetable pasta and signature dishes like the Jumbo Gumbo, BC's offers traditional options and nightly specials as well. The interior is contemporary yet warm, while the spacious patio is perfect on pleasant days and cool nights too. Visit the website for recipes, reservations, and information about private events.

(636) 542-9090
11 Meadows Circle Dr., #400
www.billcardwell.com

DONATELLI'S BISTRO
Guests will find not only an extensive menu of classic homemade Italian favorites, but a cozy yet lively atmosphere at Donatelli's. The piano bar is very popular for dining and drinks while enjoying live music, and the wine rooms are great for entertaining private parties. View the entertainment schedule on the website.

Open every day at 11 a.m.
(636) 561-6966
8653 Hwy. N
www.donatellisbistro.com

JIM & DEB'S LAKESIDE PUB
In existence for decades, some call this establishment the hidden gem of Lake St. Louis. There's constant entertainment with poker, darts, live music, karaoke, and much more. Taco Tuesday is a favorite and happy hour lasts all day long on this day of the week. Guests (including furry friends) love the huge deck, which has outdoor heaters, TVs, and umbrellas for shade. The restaurant is open seven days a week and serves breakfast on Saturday and Sunday until noon or until they run out, whichever comes first. Theme nights and the menu are posted on the website.

(636) 625-5040
10600 Veterans Memorial Pkwy.
www.jimanddebslakesidepub.com

ENTERTAINMENT/THINGS TO DO

ART AND PAINTING CLASSES
Taught by award-winning artist Marie Donato, classes like pastel, water painting, and drawing take place in city hall. Students must be a minimum of 18 years old. Fees along with the class schedule and list of needed supplies can be found on the website.

200 Civic Center Dr.
www.lakesaintlouis.com

LAKE SAINT LOUIS TRIATHLON
At more than 30 years old, this is the oldest organized triathlon in the St. Louis metropolitan area. Drawing competitors from all over the country, the event is USA Triathlon–sanctioned and competition rules apply. Participants must pick up their own packet, and non–USA Triathlon members must obtain one-day insurance. To register or for course descriptions, fees, or swim practice information, visit the website.

www.lakesaintlouis.com

NATIONAL EQUESTRIAN CENTER
If you're looking for something unique to do, visit this spectacular Midwest venue. With both indoor and outdoor

arenas, spectators can watch equestrian and dog shows, see the circus, or hold a corporate event here. The indoor facilities are always 60 degrees and provide ample bleacher seating and concessions. Equestrian shows include barrel racing, dressage, English pleasure, mounted shooting, pole bending, quarter horse, reining, rodeo roping, saddlebred, show jumping, and Western pleasure. Dog shows include agility and kennel club. There are RV and camper services on-site including chatted parking, true 20/30-amp electric, water, and dump services. For show schedules and directions, visit the website.

(636) 561-8080
6880 Lake St. Louis Blvd.
www.thenationalequestriancenter.com

POLAR PLUNGE

Often referred to as the "unbearable" event or as "freezin' for a reason," the annual Polar Plunge is held in February and benefits the Special Olympics of Missouri. Proceeds are designated for sports training and competitions for children as well as adults with intellectual disabilities. It is hosted by the Lake St. Louis, Wentzville, and O'Fallon Police Departments, in addition to the St. Charles County Sheriff's Department. There is no entry fee, but a minimum of $75 must be raised by the day of the event. Participants receive a T-shirt or higher-valued prize and can register online. Costumes are encouraged and team names and costumes must be appropriate. To register or donate and to find out more about the Polar Plunge, visit the website.

www.somo.kintera.org/plungestl

PARKS/TRAILS

BOULEVARD PARK

This picturesque 20-acre park with ponds and fountains is popular for its amphitheater, which is reserved primarily for weddings, but it is also the location of Movies in the Park during the months of May through August. The large pavilion with dusk-to-dawn lighting and electrical outlets also gets much use. In addition, there are walking paths, a playground, a volleyball net, softball and soccer fields, and a big BBQ pit. For fees and to reserve pavilions and fields, go to the website.

2550 Lake St. Louis Blvd.
www.lakesaintlouis.com

FOUNDERS PARK

A 55-acre sports complex, Founders Park has a sports-oriented theme. Along with numerous baseball diamonds and soccer fields for rent, the park has picnic facilities, walking paths, a playground, climbing stations, swings, and more. The annual Halloween Party in the Park is held here and includes a hayride, DJ, inflatables, and more. Wear your costume!

7 Freymuth Rd.
www.lakesaintlouis.com

HAWK RIDGE PARK

By far, the biggest draw at Hawk Ridge Park is Zachary's Playground, which was the first in the county to be built fully ADA accessible. The park encompasses 16.9 acres and includes a spray pad and a half-mile walking trail. The pavilion is near the playground, making it ideal for party rentals.

8392 Orf Rd.
www.lakesaintlouis.com

VETERANS MEMORIAL PARK

Veterans Memorial Park was created to honor all those who have served in the military. Flags for all branches of the service are represented. Commemorative bricks have been placed and orders for them are still being taken for $100 each. Print an order form from the website.

200 Civic Center Dr.
www.lakesaintlouis.com

TRAVELER'S TIP:

Do you have a friend or family member who lives in Lake St. Louis? Ask them to reserve your party pavilion or ball field, as residents receive discounted rates.

TRAVELER'S TIP:

While you have to score an invite from an association member to get out on the lake, visitors can sometimes catch a glimpse of the water ski show from the boulevard by the dam (I-70 side). Water skiers build human pyramids by climbing up one another's shoulders and perform other difficult tricks and maneuvers.

ST. CHARLES NEIGHBORHOODS – FAR WEST

WENTZVILLE

In 2008, Wentzville was affectionately named "Missouri's Boomtown" because of its rapid growth. It was the fastest-growing city in St. Charles County in 2010. With a population of more than 29,000 today, it's difficult to fathom that there were a mere 5,000 residents back in 1990. The city was founded in 1855, when many began settling in the area and the railroad was pushing across the state. Landowner William M. Allen donated a tract of land along the railroad right-of-way to build a station for community use. This not only increased the number of settlers that came to the area, but also provided services to those already living there. Wentzville officially became a city in 1872. Because the city grew so quickly, it is an obvious mix of both old and new. Visitors exiting I-70 onto Wentzville Parkway will find an abundance of modern restaurants and shopping opportunities, while many original buildings are still home to local businesses and eateries in the downtown area. From unique events like the Renaissance Faire to fun outdoor activities such as paintball, in addition to shopping, parks, and places to eat, there's a little bit of everything awaiting those visiting this continuously growing city. (All locations are in Wentzville unless otherwise noted.)

SHOPPING

ANN'S BRA SHOP

With a large inventory and the ability to order, shoppers will find a super-wide range of sizes in an abundance of styles and fashionable colors at Ann's Bra Shop. The knowledgeable staff provides personal service to customers with a need for bridal, plus size, mastectomy, and countless other styles of bras. In addition, shoppers can purchase swimwear and cover-ups as well as sleep and loungewear here.

Monday through Wednesday and Friday, 10 a.m.–6 p.m.
Thursday, 10 a.m.–8 p.m.
Saturday, 10 a.m.–5 p.m.
Closed Sunday
(636) 332-6700
974 Wentzville Pkwy.
www.brashop.com

AVA'S CLOSET

For new and quality used pieces for kids and teens, visit Ava's Closet. Personalized wooden signs and handcrafted items like blankets, headbands, and bows are also popular selling items. In addition, the shop hosts birthday parties and classes with headband and bow-making. Mom's Night Out is a big hit too. For more information, log on to the website.

(636) 327-8687
1843 W Pearce Blvd.
www.avascloset.org

BACKYARD RESALE & ANTIQUES

Shoppers can find antiques and quality resale merchandise, along with some home décor items here. Hours are limited and seasonal, so calling ahead is recommended.

(636) 327-6972
5011 Hwy. P
Find Backyard Resale & Antiques on Facebook

FIRESIDE TREASURES

Take a walk down memory lane at Fireside Treasures where you'll find high-end antiques and fine collectibles, as well as good conversation. In business with her daughter-in-law, Bonnie has been antiquing for 50 years and carries large pieces that are truly old and hold a history, in addition to some home décor merchandise. It's the perfect stop before or after dining, since it's just across the street from the West Allen Grill.

Wednesday through Saturday, 11 a.m.–5 p.m.
Sunday, 9 a.m.–1 p.m.
(636) 327-7377
6 W Main St.
Find Fireside Treasures on Facebook

USA RESALE

Specializing in furniture, home décor, jewelry, shoes, purses, antiques, collectibles, toys, and more, this resale shop has an inventory of quality items. They are proud supporters of the Fisher House, which assists the families of wounded and hospitalized soldiers.

Open every day except Sunday
(636) 327-7666
1251 Wentzville Pkwy.
www.usaresalellc.com

FLEA MARKET

Hosted by the Wentzville Community Club, the flea market is open every Sunday year-round except on Easter. Funds raised benefit local organizations. In addition to a variety of merchandise (there are 400 vendor spaces), the Blue Pitcher Cafe offers shoppers breakfast, lunch, and dinner items. Shoppers should note that vendors cannot always make change for purchases. For a market map, the list of menu items, and other helpful information, visit the website.

(636) 327-6358
500 W Main St.
www.wentzvillecommunityclub.com

THE WOODEN DOOR

Seasonal décor such as beautifully decorated Christmas trees greets shoppers at the door, inviting them to ooh and aah through the maze of darling gift items, florals, gourmet foods, art, and handcrafted furniture. The Wooden Door also offers bridal registry.

Monday through Saturday, 10 a.m.–6 p.m. (open until 7 p.m. on Thursday)
Sunday, noon–5 p.m.
(636) 332-3888
1155 Wentzville Pkwy., Ste. 107
www.thewoodendoorhomedecor.com

RESTAURANTS/DINING

KIMBERLY'S BAKE SHOP
Sinfully delicious baked goods beckon to you from beyond the glass upon entering the shop, and cakes for all occasions are available to order too. The cupcakes are divine—delicious on the inside and topped with beautiful icing creations on the outside. Some of the most popular flavors include Wedding Cake (almond cake with raspberry filling) and the Chocolate Overload, which is just as the name suggests. However, the Elvis (banana bread with peanut butter icing, of course) and the Maple Bacon (think syrup-filled cake topped with crispy bacon crumbles) are also to die for!

(636) 327-7727
2 W Pearce Blvd.
Find Kimberly's Bake Shop on Facebook

LOS PORTALES MEXICAN RESTAURANT & GROCERY
For authentic Mexican flavor, visit Los Portales, which is part restaurant, part grocer. The fish tacos are a popular choice, but the menu is long and offers a wide variety.

(636) 639-1522
503 W Pearce Blvd.
www.losportalesmo.com

MAGGIE MALONES
Order up some Irish Nachos, sink your teeth into the house favorite, Maggie's Signature Horseshoe (turkey or hamburger on Texas toast topped with fries and cheese sauce), or just nosh on some good ol' American pub fare. Friday and Saturday bring live music, and diners can play pool or darts or sing karaoke. At Maggie Malones, the food is freshly prepared and the service is friendly. Log on to the website for the music schedule and to see the long list of specials.

(636) 332-1176
990 Wentzville Pkwy.
www.maggiemaloneswentzville.com

STEFANINA'S ITALIAN RESTAURANT

Mostly known for their pizza, Stefanina's dough is made daily, then topped with fresh vegetables and herbs (some of which they grow themselves). They make all their sauces and grind their own cheese. In addition to pizza, they offer steak, shrimp, pasta dishes, appetizers, soup, salad, gelato, and much more. A banquet room, catering, carryout, and take & bakes are available too.

(636) 327-5800
762 W Pearce Blvd.
www.stefaninas-wentzville.com

SUNNY STREET CAFE

Traditional breakfast choices such as hash browns and syrupy pancakes, along with those with a kick like the chorizo breakfast tacos await diners. The quiche of the day is always a good pick, along with the grilled veggie flatbread, bistro burger, or Bavarian melt. Other palate-pleasing options include sandwiches, wraps, soup, and fresh salads, while protein wraps and gluten-free and lighter options are available for the more health-conscious guest. Breakfast and lunch are both offered all day.

6:30 a.m.–2:30 p.m.
(636) 639-7473
1814 Wentzville Pkwy.
www.sunnystreetcafe.com

THE TATTOOED DOG

Self-described as "Upscale Dive Grub" in a larger version of the original Burger Ink. Food Truck, the Tattooed Dog restaurant serves appetizers, burgers, sandwiches, salads, and more, but it kicks it up a notch by turning the expected into the unexpected. By adding a twist to each menu item, a signature dish is created.

Tuesday through Thursday, 11 a.m.–8 p.m.
Friday and Saturday, 11 a.m.–9 p.m.
(636) 887-2178
403 Luetkenhaus Blvd.
www.thetattooeddog.com

TEXAS SMOKEHOUSE SALOON

Everything is bigger in Texas, and there's no exception with the Terrible Texan. Finish this signature sandwich and you'll earn a free cocktail of your choice (must be at least 21 years old to enter the contest). Sink your teeth into an artisan roll filled with smoked sausage, pork, brisket, chicken, and bacon, topped with pepper jack cheese, onion frazzles, firebug sauce, fresh jalapeños, and onions. All meats are smoked in-house daily. Other menu items include Jacked Up Tator Tots, the Texas Smokehouse Nachos, chili, pizza, steaks, and more.

For entertainment there are TVs, pool tables, and live music on Fridays and Saturdays.

(636) 332-3626
909 Main Plaza Dr.
www.texasmokehouseandsaloon.com

UNKORKED WINE GARDEN

Guests love the yummy salads, wraps, starters, and paninis, while the relaxing patio area keeps them lingering for hours. Both covered and uncovered seating is available and space heaters keep diners toasty on cooler days. This is the perfect place to unwind over some wine and a bite to eat, but it's also a popular choice for events as well. The patio is king, but indoor seating is an option when the weather isn't agreeable. UnKorked Wine Garden sits next door to the post office.

(636) 887-4141
205 E Allen St.
www.unkorkedwinegarden.com

WENTZVILLE DONUT CAFE

The huge selection of donuts is made from quality ingredients and classic recipes, in addition to new and original flavors. Guests can also order breakfast sandwiches, biscuits & gravy, and other bakery items, including cakes.

5 a.m.–noon daily
(636) 332-2241
714 W Pearce Blvd.
www.thedonutcafe.com

WEST ALLEN GRILL

Customers have been known to line up down the block to get a taste of the famous ribs, sizzling fajitas, or other tasty options offered at the West Allen Grill. While diners might have trouble deciding what to order, there is no shortage of dishes to choose from. With steaks, seafood, burgers, and everything in between, you'll want to keep coming back again and again. Perusing the historic art on the walls is a good distraction for drooling mouths while waiting for orders.

(636) 327-3030
9 W Allen St.
www.westallengrill.net

PLACES TO STAY

FAIRFIELD INN & SUITES
Sitting just off I-70 at Exit 208 and only a few minutes from I-40, this hotel is conveniently located and super easy for travelers to find. Amenities include a complimentary hot breakfast and turn-down service, and guests can also utilize the pool or exercise room.

(636) 332-5000
130 Crossroads South Dr.
www.marriott.com

ENTERTAINMENT/THINGS TO DO

BEAR CREEK GOLF COURSE
Also referred to as "The Home of the Grizzly," this premier public golfing facility located amidst beautiful surroundings was the first 18-hole course within the city of Wentzville. The championship-style construction was designed to preserve the natural habitat and most of the trees in the area, creating a one-of-a-kind look and unique features at each hole. In addition to tournaments, Bear Creek hosts weddings and other events. For multiple daily rates and additional information, visit the website.

(636) 332-5018
158 Bear Creek Dr.
www.bearcreekgolf.com

LINDENWOOD ICE ARENA
Open for public skating, the facility also has an arcade and is available for group and party rental. In addition, the

Lindenwood Lions hockey (men's and women's) and the synchronized skating teams compete here. To learn more and see a current schedule of events, log on to the website.

(636) 627-6700
910 Main Plaza
www.icearena.lindenwood.edu.

kids

PLAYTIME PARTY CENTER

Tons of indoor fun awaits at Playtime Party Center. With inflatables, roller skating, games, and concessions, it's the perfect place for kids to hold a party or just burn off some energy. Socks are required and can be purchased at the counter. Visit the website for package pricing, a virtual tour, and a list of menu items.

Monday through Thursday, 10 a.m.–9 p.m.
Friday and Saturday, 10 a.m.–10 p.m.
Sunday, 11 a.m.–8 p.m.
(636) 887-4244
1225 Wentzville Pkwy.
www.playtimepartycenter.com

kids

WACKY WARRIORS PAINTBALL

Providing fast-paced action and fun for kids and adults too, Wacky Warriors Paintball offers 18 playing fields, including woods-ball, air-ball, and the two-story castle field, to name a few. All paint must be purchased through Wacky Warriors, but goggles, paintball guns, and all other equipment is available to rent there. The facilities are open year-round for open play, in addition to group events and for parties. Everyone must sign a waiver to participate, but spectators are welcome. Visit the website for pricing, age requirements, a calendar of events, and package deals.

(315) 518-4436
700 Wacky Rd.
www.wackywarriors.com

kids

FESTIVALS/EVENTS

ST LOUIS RENAISSANCE FAIRE

The Renaissance Faire is an immersive, living history event that allows participants to travel back in time to 16th-century France. Fairgoers are treated to events of the period as well as food and drink. Merchants sell items to bring the time period alive. There is entertainment as well as contests. Everyone is invited to dress for the times. There is an admission fee for this annual event.

Rotary Park, Wentzville
(800) 373-0357
info@STLrenfest.com
www.STLrenfest.com

kids

WABASH DAYS FESTIVAL

Celebrating the importance of railroads in Wentzville's history, this annual three-day street festival takes place in August. Appropriately held along Allen and Main Streets, parallel to the still-active train tracks, it offers a plethora of fun for the entire family. Activities include a BBQ competition, a run, motorcycle and car shows, vendors, carnival rides, booths, live concerts, inflatables, and food, in addition to a Miss Missouri pageant. Aside from the fun, the best part is that much of it is FREE! Visit the website for the schedule of events.

www.wentzvillemo.org

kids

PARKS/TRAILS/POOLS

Wentzville has some of the best parks in the county, with popular features such as fields and courts, but also unique attractions like the new water park at the Aquatic Center. In addition, some offer movie and concert nights at no charge. A complete list of Wentzville city parks along with what each has to offer can be found at www.wentzvillemo.org. In addition, the "Fun Times" publication, published three times a year, is posted here and can be downloaded to see current happenings. County park information is available at www.sccmo.org.

TRAVELER'S TIP:

Watch for two new up-and-coming parks that will have both typical park attractions as well as modern features. Both city parks are in the funding stage and will be constructed in phases. The Heartland Park will be at William Dierberg Drive and will include riparian landscape, detention lakes, a wildlife enhancement area, and much more. The Peruque Valley Park is considered a diamond in the rough in its current state of wetlands, meadows, and wildlife settings. Plans include a paved backbone trail along with natural trails, creek overlooks, adventure areas, a lake and boardwalk, and environmental meadows, in addition to other features. A complete list of this park's future features along with the conceptual design map for Heartland Park can be found by clicking Parks and Recreation under the Departments tab at www.wentzvillemo.org.

BICENTENNIAL PARK

The Memorial Garden Park, which honors the Declaration of Independence of 1776 and the Civil War battle that took place nearby in 1861 between traveling Union soldiers and Missouri bushwhackers, is here.

22 W Pearce Blvd.
www.wentzvillemo.org

BROEMMELSIEK PARK

This 494-acre county park offers a bevy of things for park goers to do. The 4.7-acre off-leash dog park has a long dock for running and jumping into the pond. It was voted best dog park in the region and the annual Paws in the Park event is held here. There are seven-plus miles of multiuse trails, which can be used for horseback riding, hiking, and biking, as well as equipped lakes for fishing, and a historic agricultural education area. The Astronomy Site was the first of its kind in St. Charles County. It is free and offers nine paved stations, each with 20-amp electrical service. Each Friday, beginning at dusk (weather permitting), the Astronomical Society of Eastern Missouri holds public viewings. Named for Jack Broemmelsiek, the park has a visitors center under construction on the grounds where he and his family lived for more than 30 years. Go to the county's website for a map of the park and a list of its facilities, rules and regulations, and to find current trail closures.

1615 Schwede Rd.
www.sccmo.org

INDIAN CAMP CREEK PARK

At 603 acres, this is the largest park in St. Charles County. Unique features include an observation tower where visitors can climb to the top of the grain silo and look out over the countryside, a homestead, and the Cannon Family Cemetery with headstones dating back to the 19th century. In addition, there are 10 miles of multiuse trails, a stocked fishing lake, 18-hole disc golf, an eco-playground, picnic facilities, and youth group camping facilities.

2679 Dietrich Rd., Foristell
www.sccmo.org

QUAIL RIDGE PARK

Home to the National Horseshoe Pitchers Hall of Fame, Quail Ridge Park offers visitors the Hall of Fame museum and even a game of horseshoes in this huge indoor facility. The 250-acre park includes over seven miles of trails connecting to park amenities and through woods, which are ideal for viewing native flora and wildlife. The lake and pond are both stocked for fishing and there's a disc golf course. Quail Ridge Lodge is popular for large groups or wedding parties and was voted by local brides as the Best Wedding Destination. Adjacent to the lodge is a large picnic area and a gazebo, often used for exchanging vows and lakeside photos. In addition, there's a large area with shelters, BBQ pits, a playground, restrooms, water and electric sources, and a hard surface plaza grouped together for big group use. Other favorites of the park include hayrides and the 1.5-acre off-leash dog area.

5501 Quail Ridge Pkwy.
www.sccmo.org

ROTARY PARK

The largest park in the area is Rotary Park in nearby Foristell. With 72 acres of scenic beauty, it is utilized for many local festivities, including the Greater St. Louis Renaissance Faire, the St. Charles County Fair, and the Holiday Night Lights. There's an amphitheater, several pavilions, an exhibit hall, a playground, and a 1.3-mile pedestrian trail, in addition to a 5-acre fishing lake.

2577 Meyer Rd., Foristell
www.wentzvillemo.org

SPLASH STATION AQUATIC CENTER

This new state-of-the-art water park is every kid's dream. With a water flume, lazy river, water basketball, a children's splash playground, wet deck spray ground, a diving platform, and concessions, you'll have to drag the kids out when it's time to go. In addition, there's a zero beach entry, lap lanes, a water shade structure, pavilions, and a therapy seat and water benches. The Pooch Plunge, a fun swim for people and their pups, is held here and includes a snack for each dog and door prizes. Preregistration is required at least one week prior to the event and owners must provide proof of vaccinations. Dogs must be leashed when out of the water. There is a fee of $10 for nonresidents and a discounted price of $8 for residents.

(636) 327-5104
1141 Peine Rd., Wentzville
www.wentzvillemo.org

TOWNE PARK

Unique for its combination of history, nature, and educational qualities, this park is located in nearby Foristell. The St. Charles County Parks Department won the 2007 McReynolds Award from the Missouri Alliance for Historic Preservation and was recognized at the Missouri State Capitol in Jefferson City for the effort they put forth to restore the historic 1800s homestead on the site, formerly known as the Pink Plantation. Another special quality of this park is the Certified Nature Explore Classroom, which encompasses 11 learning stations including wildflower, nature art, water, and sand play areas, just to name a few. Many classes visit this park, and special events and tours are popular attractions too. In addition, there are picnic areas, a forest-themed playground, a large fishing pond, trails, and a series of interlinked scenic rain gardens.

100 Towne Park Dr.
www.natureexplore.org

WE ALL SCREAM FOR ICE CREAM

CHILL
For yogurt your way, head to Chill, where you can order gelati and smoothies or create your own yogurt concoction or swirling parfait. Most flavors contain 20 to 35 calories per ounce and are generally low in fat and sugar. No-sugar-added varieties and dairy-free sorbets are available too. Chalkboard walls, colorful furniture, and bright décor provide a fun atmosphere that's appealing to everyone. Log on to the website for nutritional information or to find out how to get a free mix on your birthday.

Open daily at noon
(636) 327-1485
1894 Wentzville Pkwy.
www.chillyogurt.com

FRITZ'S FROZEN CUSTARD
Made with fresh natural ingredients and an "old time" freezing process, Fritz's is tops when it comes to custard. With the original 90 percent fat-free vanilla, the lite 95 percent fat-free vanilla, and a no-sugar-added vanilla available, even diabetics and those counting calories can indulge. The rich, full-bodied chocolate is always an option too, in addition to the flavor of the day. Order up your favorite custard treat or purchase some to take home. You can find Fritz's in O'Fallon and St. Peters too. For a list of menu items and the Flavor of the Day calendar, as well as seasonal hours, log on to the website.

(636) 639-8088
1105 W Pearce Blvd.
www.fritzsfrozencustard.com

LULU'S SHAVED ICE

Concretes, floats, sundaes, and more made with frozen yogurt and custard, shaved ice, pie, and quarts to go are offered here. In addition, LuLu's Shaved Ice is available for event and party rentals in its mobile station. LuLu's even caters to canines with shaved ice in beef or chicken flavor. Hours are seasonal, so calling ahead is suggested. A list of flavors along with the full menu can be found at the website.

(314) 691-6062
904 Main Plaza Dr.
www.lulusshavedice.com

SMOOTHIE KING

The original inventor of the smoothie bar and the founder of Smoothie King began blending real fruit with nutrients and protein to improve health and fight food allergies way back in 1973. Since 1989, Smoothie King has been named the No. 1 franchise in its category 20 times by *Entrepreneur* magazine, and it's easy to see why. It's a teenager's dream and the perfect adult meal replacement or snack too. With Chobani Greek Yogurt smoothies, enhancers like muscle builders and protein, immune boosters, and supplements, to name just a very few options available, every customer will find the perfect combination. Whether you want to slim down, bulk up, or just delight in a sweet treat, visit Smoothie King seven days a week.

(636) 856-1660
1861 Wentzville Pkwy.
www.smoothieking.com

ST. CHARLES NEIGHBORHOODS – SOUTHWEST

AUGUSTA/DEFIANCE/NEW MELLE

The charming little towns that make up St. Charles County's wine country offer stunning river views, local artisans, rolling hills, and quaint lodgings, along with big business. Once focused only on the production of their local harvests, most wineries are now offering their customers a full winery experience, encouraging them to stay a while to enjoy their wine in a relaxed atmosphere of beautiful scenery often with gourmet foods, and even musical entertainment. Wine country is the perfect getaway and has become quite popular for weddings, just-the-girls trips, and romantic outings, as well as for those biking the Katy Trail. In addition to wineries, there are cute shops, annual events, delectable food options, and numerous outdoor activities for guests to enjoy. For a list of businesses within the area and other helpful information, visit www.augusta-chamber.org or www.augusta-missouri.com.

RESTAURANTS/DINING/WINERIES

AUGUSTA BREWING CO.
The scenic hillside is the best place here to sip a cold crafted brew, but there's covered seating too. Live music and the Missouri River view add to the relaxing atmosphere. Augusta Brewing Co. has limited hours in the off-season.

(636) 482-2337
5521 Water St., Augusta
www.augustabrewing.com

There's live music here on the weekends from April to October. This is the perfect place to sit back and relax with the favorite from your tasting.

(636) 228-4301, x24
5601 High St., Augusta
www.augustawinery.com

AUGUSTA WINERY
Fun gifts, wine recipes, and award-winning bottles of wine line the walls and await tasters. The attached wine terrace is shaded with greenery and is perfect for warm days. The spacious wine and beer garden is beautiful too, simply decorated with a Tuscan fountain and pergola.

BALDUCCI VINEYARDS
Overlooking 76 acres of vineyards and farmland, Balducci Vineyards offers live music, award-winning food, and spectacular wine selections. There's lots of open hillside seating and covered areas too. Visit year-round every day of the week.

(636) 482-8466
6601 Hwy. 94 S, three miles west of Augusta
www.balduccivineyards.com

CAFÉ ANGELINA
Located inside Frisella Nursery in Defiance, visitors can enjoy breakfast or lunch amidst the gorgeous plants and flowers on the lovely covered patio or inside the nursery. Take time to browse unique gift and garden items and take in the beautifully landscaped property before or after dining. Café hours are limited in the off-season.

(636) 798-2555
550 Hwy. F, Defiance
www.frisellanursery.com

CHANDLER HILL VINEYARDS
Upon the deeded grounds once owned by former slave Joseph Chandler, expansive vaulted ceilings with warm wooden beams lend charm to the indoor space at Chandler Hill. The outdoor deck and patio areas are even more exquisite, with picturesque views of rolling hills and countryside. Enjoy live music over a meal and your favorite wine, or just catch up with friends at this delightful Defiance winery.

(636) 798-2675
596 Defiance Rd., Defiance
www.chandlerhillvineyards.com

DEFIANCE ROADHOUSE
Popular for bikers (motor and otherwise), this establishment offers visitors a change of scenery along with their food and favorite beverage. There's lots of seating outdoors and live music Friday through Sunday.

(636) 987-2075
2999 Hwy. 94 S, Defiance
www.defianceroadhouse.net

FIRESIDE BAR & GRILL
Offering burgers, wings, and specials like lasagna, as well as other home-cooked American dishes, this establishment also has live entertainment and is open daily.

(636) 828-1189
30 West Hwy. D, Ste. 103, New Melle
Find Fireside Bar & Grill on Facebook

GRAPEVINE WINE BISTRO & VISITOR'S CENTER

In addition to elegant wines, a large beer selection, and friendly service, the Grapevine Wine Bistro serves a wide range of plates to please any palate, including gourmet hot dogs, homemade oven pizza, and signature sandwiches like the Croque Madame Ham & Gruyere, as well as soup, salad, and desserts. Each Thursday from 5 p.m. to 9 p.m. diners can indulge in the chef's handcrafted special (reservations are recommended) and there's live entertainment on Saturday and Sunday afternoons. The inside is inviting and cozy, but the front patio is lovely too. Visitors can also obtain local information about the wine country here. Open Thursday through Sunday, seasonally.

(636) 798-2400
2886 S Hwy. 94, Defiance, adjacent to the Vera Jacobsen Park
www.grapevinewinebistro.com

HOLY GRAIL WINERY

The Holy Grail is a newer establishment in Augusta, but the owner has been making wine for over 30 years. The inside is a bit small, but there's an outdoor patio too. Bring your picnic basket, sip some wine, and indulge in a sweet treat from the chocolate bar. Holy Grail Winery is open on Saturdays and Sundays.

(636) 221-7604
5505 Locust St., Augusta, across from the Uptown Store
www.holygrailwinery.com

KATE'S COFFEE HOUSE

This quaint 1905 home with stained glass windows, a brick patio, and charming courtyard invites guests of Kate's to come in and stay awhile. Aside from variations of rich coffee, they serve breakfast, lunch, smoothies, and sweet ice cream. The coffee house is open daily until 3 p.m.

(636) 482-4022
5525 Walnut St., Augusta, in Oak's Crossing just up from the Katy Trail
www.oakscrossing-augusta.com

LIZ'S BAR & GRILL

Dating back to 1926, when it was built as a general store, this building is now home to Liz's Bar & Grill. Grab a burger, drink a cold one, or get your hair cut from the barber in the back at this must-see, one-of-a-kind establishment. While in town, head down the street to see one of the oldest buildings still standing in New Melle today. Built in 1857, this historic building at 3669 Mill Street features an old gable front and was once the Meier General Store.

(636) 828-5497
3585 Mill St., New Melle
Find Liz's Bar & Grill on Facebook

MONTELLE WINERY

Sip on some Himmelswein (it means "heaven's wine" in German), grab a bite from Klondike Cafe, and find a sweet spot on one of the many outdoor decks where you can look out over miles and miles of beautiful rolling hills. The tasting room is lively and encompasses the cafe, tasting bar, and an array of gift items. Just beyond the door awaits a peaceful setting with breathtaking views. On the way out, buy a bottle for later and a Starbucks coffee (brilliant!) for the drive.

(636) 228-4464
201 Montelle Dr. at Hwy. 94, Augusta
www.montelle.com

MOUNT PLEASANT ESTATES

Offering guests much more than just wine, there's an abundance of outdoor space with breathtaking views. The Appellation Cafe serves up tasty sandwiches and more, while the tasting room has a contemporary feel with endless choices. An original structure on the property (built in 1881) is now home to the Crush Lounge, which can be rented for special occasions along with the ballroom and other areas at the winery. The Arbor overlooks miles of river valley and is extremely popular for weddings and picture taking. This expansive property is open daily and is perfect for every occasion.

(636) 482-9463
5634 High St., Augusta
www.mountpleasant.com

NOBOLEIS VINEYARDS

Specializing in estate wines, Noboleis Vineyards offers stunning views, a full cafe menu of delicious appetizers, salads, burgers, specialty pizza, and more. The winery is open every day of the week year-round and has live music on the weekends from May through October. It is well worth a visit to this newer establishment in wine country.

(636) 482-4500
100 Hemsath Rd., Augusta
www.noboleisvineyards.com

PIAZZA DELI & PIZZERIA

You can fill up on pizza, sandwiches, stromboli, baked desserts, ice cream, or one of the many other choices at Piazza Deli & Pizzeria. Gluten-free crust is available along with a weight-watchers menu. Dine in or take it with you.

(636) 398-3354
1312 Hwy. DD, Defiance
www.piazzadeli.com

POP A WHEELIE ON THE KATY TRAIL

Stop by Pop A Wheelie for a sweet ice cream treat. Just off the Katy Trail, it is also the location for Tuesday Night at the Trailhead where locals and visitors gather for fun themes, entertainment, and creative foods.

5533 Water St. next to Katy Bike Rental's Augusta location

kids 🐾

SEVEN STONES WEINGARTEN

It's hard to believe that this contemporary and fully restored wine garden was once just a log structure built in 1860 by German settlers to serve as the first schoolhouse in New Melle. Lush green grounds and outdoor patios along with beautiful spacious indoor areas invite guests to engage in conversation, listen to live music, and sip their favorite wines. Special events such as Sip & Paint, Murder Mystery dinners, and yoga classes can all be enjoyed here. Seven Stones Weingarten is open Thursday through Sunday.

(636) 828-5300
4612 Hwy. Z, New Melle
www.sevenstoneswine.com

SUGAR CREEK WINERY

This winery encompasses a Victorian home used for indoor seating and tasting, a gazebo where entertainers perform live music and weddings frequently take place, and a spacious covered deck and grounds providing lovely views of the Missouri River Valley and vineyards. Gifts and light snacks of cheese and sausage can be purchased here. The winery is open daily, year-round from 10:30 a.m. to 5:30 p.m. See the website for the entertainment schedule.

(636) 987-2400
125 Boone Country Ln., Defiance
www.sugarcreekwines.com

WINE COUNTRY GARDENS

One of the first wineries visitors encounter upon entering wine country is also a favorite for obvious reasons. The expansive grounds contain fountains, gardens, waterfalls, and stunning views. There's yummy food, friendly service, gift items for purchase, and of course, superb wine. Spacious outdoor areas, including patios and decks, and gorgeous grounds, make Wine Country Gardens a popular choice for weddings and other special events. A covered seating area accommodates 320 guests. This winery is open from late March through November from 10 a.m. to 5 p.m.

(636) 798-2288
2711 S Hwy. 94, Defiance
www.winecountrygardens.net

YELLOW FARMHOUSE WINERY

The big hill overlooking the Missouri River Valley at Yellow Farmhouse Winery is popular on warm summer days and on movie nights when pizza is brought in. It's fun in the fall too. Guests are welcome to bring a picnic basket, but light snacks are available inside.

(314) 409-6139
100 Defiance Rd., Defiance, just across the street from the Katy Trail
www.yellowfarmhousewines.com

FESTIVALS/EVENTS

CANDLELIGHT CHRISTMAS WALK
Luminaries line the streets while the charming sound of horse-drawn carriages can be heard throughout town. Visit with Santa, warm up by the toasty bonfire at the old town square where chestnuts are roasting, and hop aboard the trolley to visit local restaurants, wineries, and shops. This old-fashioned Christmas celebration has been a favorite for more than 30 years.

Historic Downtown Augusta
www.augusta-chamber.org

FALL HARVEST FESTIVAL
A scavenger hunt and other children's activities with prizes, along with pumpkin patch rides, music, art, and locally grown and made wines are favorites at this festival. There's a picnic and concert on Friday night, followed by a winemaker social on Saturday. Reserve your spot, as seating is limited.

Augusta
(636) 228-4005
www.augusta-chamber.org

PLEIN AIR ART FESTIVAL
A celebration of the energy and beauty of springtime, this festival draws over 100 artists to the Augusta-Defiance area. Upon rolling hills at wineries, atop river bluffs, and anywhere else they find inspiration, artists paint and create their works of art outdoors in the open air. Unique and interesting events are scheduled at various locations throughout town and the artists' work is judged at this annual event. To meet the artists and view this year's schedule of events, visit the website.

www.augustapleinair.com

SWINGIN' IN THE VINES
Board the pumpkin wagon to Hoeft Vineyard where you'll sample local wines in a 130-year-old vaulted wine cellar. Then pick up your harvest basket that includes a bottle of wine and gourmet picnic items. Find a comfy hay bale and stay awhile for musical entertainment. Additional wine can be purchased and water is complimentary. This annual event is super popular and has sold out for the last eight years. Make your reservations early.

Augusta
(636) 228-4005
www.augusta-chamber.org.

PLACES TO STAY

APPLE GATE INN B&B
The perfect balance of privacy and attentive service, along with charm and elegance, keeps guests returning to this early American style bed and breakfast. It was built in 1865 and sits just a block from the Katy Trail. Each of the three rooms has its own private entrance and bath and is a little different from the others. Some of the unique features include a sauna (that can be used with steam too), a dual shower head for two, a jetted tub, a balcony, a kitchenette, and gas fireplaces. Pictures of the rooms along with descriptions and pricing for each can be found on the website. The grounds are lovely too, with floral landscaping, a bonfire area, and quaint sitting spaces. In addition, a full-service, three-course breakfast is included. The B&B is open Wednesday through Sunday but is closed in January.

(636) 228-4248
5549 Main St., Augusta
www.applegate-inn.com

AUGUSTA WINE COUNTRY INN
Between the Edelweiss Guest House B&B (a German-style Gasthaus with six jacuzzi suites) and the inn, which is two blocks away, there are nine suites for guests to choose from. The inn offers a romantic ambiance with a veranda and spectacular sunsets. Log on to the website to reserve a room that suits your style and fits your needs. Both properties are located in Augusta.

(636) 482-4307
Wine Country Inn
5619 Fifth St.
Edelweiss Guest House & Luxury Suites
5567 Walnut St.
www.augustawinecountry.com

THE CONSERVATORY GUEST COTTAGE

A comfortable mix of old and new, the unique décor in the Conservatory features salvaged cross beams, a vaulted ceiling, a sunny sitting space, and cozy sleeping quarters. The property is located just a few blocks from Oaks Crossing.

(636) 288-4072
245 Lower St., Augusta
www.oakscrossing-augusta.com

GRAPEVINE VACATION RENTALS

With three different tastefully decorated luxurious properties, it will be hard to choose where to stay. The first has anything and everything a guest could possibly want. The 4 bedroom/2 bath home sleeps 10 and has a private patio, tiki bar, jacuzzi, pool, and wraparound deck. The kitchen has all that you need to prepare your own meal, but you can't go wrong by dining at Grapevine Wine Bistro. The Hackmann House has 3 bedrooms plus a sleeping loft and 2 baths. There's a hot tub, a 2-story deck, and a gas grill. The smallest property is a 2 bedroom/1 bath that sleeps 6 and has a hot tub. To see pictures of the properties or to reserve one, log on to the website.

(636) 598-2163
2886 S Hwy. 94, Defiance
www.grapevinevacationrentals.com

GREATVIEW BED & BREAKFAST

An unusual sight in wine country, this bed & breakfast is super modern and rightfully named. Offering majestic views, 3 guest suites (and more upon special request), an outdoor kitchen with grill, an in-ground pool, and hot tub, guests may never want to leave. Relaxing outdoor seating by the fire pit, on the covered patio, and around the pool allow for large group gatherings. In addition, the pool table, library area, and seating in front of the fireplace allow everyone to do their own thing while still spending time together. Reservations can be made year-round. Log on to the website for descriptions and pictures of this magnificent property and to make reservations.

(314) 581-4643 or (314) 581-4641
55 Greatview Lane, Defiance
www.greatviewbandb.com

H. S. CLAY HOUSE

Built in 1885, this Victorian charmer has 2 suites, a guest cottage, and 3 guest rooms for visitors to choose from. The innkeepers pride themselves on being attentive and creating a unique and full experience for their guests. Breakfast is served each morning along with appetizers in the evening. Some features of the guest quarters include private sitting rooms and baths, fireplaces, and balconies. Descriptions of each along with pictures can be viewed on the website. Outdoor comforts include a fire pit, hot tub, pool, wraparound porch, and numerous cozy spots to relax and enjoy the lush grounds. Reservations can be made online.

(314) 504-4203
219 Public St., Augusta
www.hsclayhouse.com

THE INN AT DEFIANCE

Choose from Norton's Nook, Cab's Corner, or Riesling's Retreat (all of which have a queen-size bed), or reserve the Vidal Blanc Suite, which has a king-size bed, sitting area, and jetted tub. All rooms have private baths, flat-screen smart TVs, robes, slippers, and private entries. Common areas include a large spa in the Four Seasons room, a lounge, fireplaces, an observation area, library, deck, and gathering space. Green amenities as well as local products and organic foods are provided for guests. This boutique B&B requires a two-night minimum on weekends, and rates are seasonal.

(636) 987-2002
125 Defiance Rd., Defiance
www.thedefianceinn.com

THE JEFFERSON GUEST HOUSE B&B

Charm and beauty abound in this beautifully restored home, ideally located just down the street from the other Stone Ledge properties and across from Kate's Coffee House. The modern and super-spacious kitchen is balanced with fine vintage décor in the sitting room and elegance in the bedroom. An enclosed porch gives guests a cozy space for cooler or rainy days, while the charming front porch with swing is the perfect space to unwind. A cozy patio off the bonus room is a lovely spot to read or just enjoy garden surroundings. Call to reserve one of the three suites in Augusta offered through Stone Ledge Properties.

(636) 233-5347 or (314) 971-1823
5524 Walnut St., Augusta
www.jeffersonguesthouse.com

KLONDIKE PARK

Primitive and basic tent sites, along with cabins, are available for year-round camping. However, the shower and flushing toilets are not accessible from November 1 to March 31 (these dates are subject to change as they are weather dependent). Log on to the website for park information, rules, and maps.

(636) 949-7535
4600 Hwy. 94, Augusta
www.sccmo.org

MISS ELLIE'S GARDEN INN

The perfect mix of elegant and shabby chic with all the modern conveniences, Miss Ellie's Garden Inn is an absolute treasure! It's spacious yet cozy inside, but just as spectacular on the outside. There's a large screened-in porch with access to the outdoors as well as from the bedroom. The patio, complete with a pergola and fireplace, beckon to you for morning coffee or to relax after a fun day in wine country. The kitchen is stocked with everything you need if you decide to cook, but fresh-baked goodies, plates of gourmet snacks, and beverages welcome guests upon arrival. The clawfoot tub and modern shower are the perfect balance of old and new, while interesting touches like the wooden transom windows constantly catch your eye. Miss Ellie's sleeps four and has a washer and dryer to use for longer stays.

(636) 233-5347 or (314) 971-1823
221 Lower St., Augusta
www.misselliesgardeninn.com

STONE LEDGE GUEST SUITE B&B

Nestled above the historic Uptown Store (now Stone Ledge Antiques) and adjacent to Miss Ellie's Garden Inn, this guest suite is private, bright, and airy. It's much roomier than it appears from the outside and offers guests warm, inviting spaces for good conversation and relaxing. There's a full eat-in kitchen with healthy snack options, a charming sitting room with sleeper sofa, and a quaintly decorated bedroom with a queen-size bed. The balconies are perfect for watching passersby in the streets below or to gaze out over beautiful wine country. This suite sleeps four.
Breakfast is provided.

(636) 233-5347 or (314) 971-1823
5600 Locust St., Augusta
www.stoneledgeguestsuite.com

SHOPPING

AUGUSTA EMPORIUM
Shop the unique mix of antiques, collectibles, and other interesting merchandise.

(636) 228-4024
5595 Walnut St., Augusta

AUGUSTA GLASS STUDIO
Elegant hand-blown glass creations can be viewed only through the window unless you make an appointment or visit the studio during a demo or a major holiday event. Artists Sam Stang and Kaeko Maehata shape one-of-a-kind pieces, which can be found all over the country. For scheduled events, visit the website or call for an appointment.

(636) 228-4732
5508 Locust, Augusta
www.samstang.com
www.kaekomaehata.com

AUGUSTA WOOD LTD.
At Augusta Wood Ltd., shoppers find beautifully crafted furniture made from rustic cherry, brown maple, and quarter-sawn oak. The shop features unique artwork from local and nationally known artists, as well as other home décor. Decorating services are also available. The store offers delivery within 60 miles.

Monday through Saturday, 10 a.m.–5 p.m.
(636) 228-4406
5558 Walnut St., Augusta
www.augustawoodltd.com

JOHANN'S GENERAL STORE

As the only convenience store nearby, the inventory here contains a little bit of everything. Visitors can pick up some groceries, ice, fishing equipment, toiletries, and necessities, or use the ATM, copy, and fax services. The store is open daily until 6 p.m., but gasoline and diesel is conveniently available 24 hours a day at the outdoor pumps. Outdoor vending machines are accessible after the store closes as well. Call ahead for hours.

(636) 228-4500
225 Jackson St., Augusta, just up from Halcyon Spa

ROBIN'S NEST ON THE KATY TRAIL

Robin's Nest is accessible from both the highway or the Katy Trail. A boutique with adorable gift items ranging from sangria mix and gourmet foods to jewelry, scarves, and wine glasses, Robin's Nest is located in the historic Schiermeier General Store next to KATY Bike Rental in Defiance. Call ahead to be sure they are open.

(636) 223-3423
2998 S Hwy. 94, Defiance
www.robinsnestonthekatytrail.com

STONE LEDGE ANTIQUES

Located in the Uptown Store (originally the town's general store), shoppers will find more than 5,000 square feet of inventory, including unique antiques dating back to the 1800s, fine collectibles, home décor, elegant furniture, clothing, and much, much more. Some items can be previewed on the website.

Wednesday through Sunday,
11 a.m.–5 p.m.
(314) 971-1823
5606 Locust St., Augusta
www.stoneledgeantiques.com

PARKS/TRAILS

KLONDIKE PARK
Klondike Park has an amphitheater, conference center, play area, bird area, overlook, picnic shelters, fishing lake, herpetology pond, and trails for hiking and biking. There are cabins as well as primitive and basic camping options. This park also has restrooms, a shower house, and a council ring. For a map of the park and additional information, go to the website.

4600 Hwy. 94 S, Augusta
www.sccmo.org

MATSON HILL PARK
This park is favorited by mountain bikers due to its challenging natural surface trails. No ATVs or horses are allowed in the park. It encompasses 475 acres and has three trails and an interpretive exhibit on the Boone family. The Boone Trace Eastern Trailhead Marker can also be found in this area. It's just off Hwy. 94 at Matson Hill Rd. and is recognizable by the sitting area under big shady trees by the marker.

670 Matson Hill Rd., Defiance
www.sccmo.org

MISSOURI DEPARTMENT OF CONSERVATION

MDC DISCOVER nature FAMILIES

FROG GIGGING CLINIC

Monday, July 7th, 2014
6:00 PM-Midnight
August A. Busch Memorial
Conservation Area
2360 Highway D, St. Charles, MO

Register by calling:
636-441-4554

Join the staff of the Missouri Dept. of Conservation for an exciting and educational experience in frog gigging. Participants will learn the basics of frog gigging safety, equipment, identification, regulations and much more. This program will consist of classroom lessons followed by a field trip. Discover Nature – Families programs are designed to help adults & children explore nature & master outdoor skills together. This program is open to youth ages 11 to 15 and their parent or adult mentor.

discover nature family programs...

THE MISSOURI DEPARTMENT OF CONSERVATION

With family programs like frog gigging, a shooting range, and an outdoor education center, interesting exhibits, and an abundance of free materials including maps and magazines about local conservation areas, trails, fishing lakes, and other surrounding nature settings, the regional office of the Missouri Department of Conservation is well worth the stop. Kids will want to spend some time here looking at pictures, browsing the gift shop, and participating in current children's activities. Helpful information about popular nearby exploration areas like the Slough and Fallen Oak Nature Trail, and much more, can be found here.

(636) 441-4554
2360 Hwy. D

kids

ENTERTAINMENT/THINGS TO DO

AHOLT FARMS SEASONS OF FUN
Visit Aholt Farms for seasonal family fun like hayrides, Easter Egg hunts, barrel rides, a corn cannon, straw tunnel, face painting, pedal tractors and cars, as well as farm fresh produce and refreshments. Great photo ops abound. Call to schedule private parties. Activities are always weather permitting. For hours of operation, pricing, and directions, log on to the website.

(636) 228-4896
6133 Augusta Bottom Rd., Augusta
www.aholtfarms.com.

kids

AUGUSTA HISTORICAL MUSEUM
Built in 1861 by German settler August Sehrt, this home is one of seven in Augusta on the National Register of Historic Places. Sehrt built furniture and caskets in the downstairs workroom of his home, and also grew fruit trees and grapes. The museum showcases documents, artifacts, and occasional programs. Call ahead to check hours of operation or to schedule a tour.

Sunday, 1 p.m.–4 p.m.
(636) 228-4821 or (636) 228-4303
275 Webster St., Augusta

AUGUSTA VISITOR CENTER
Visitors can find brochures and guides to the area along with historical information at the Visitor Center. Call ahead for hours.

(636) 228-4440
5577 Walnut St., Augusta
www.missourilife.com/locations/augusta-visitor-center

CENTENNIAL FARMS
Family owned and operated since 1854, this farm and orchard business is now in its sixth generation. A 100-year-old timber-framed barn houses the market and is listed on the National Register of Historic Places. Apple picking, school tours, and fresh produce are available here. For directions, seasonal hours, and activities offered, visit the website.

(636) 228-4338
199 Jackson St., Augusta
www.centennialfarms.biz

THE CONFERENCE CENTER AT OAKS CROSSING
Thoughtful and stunning design allows a variety of events such as weddings, business meetings, showers, and private parties to be held here. There's an open kitchen, stained glass windows, wooden beams, and other unique architectural features. The grounds are decorated elegantly with arbors, fountains, and courtyards. In addition, Maggie and Myrtle's Flower Shop is on-site and can provide centerpieces, bouquets, or other floral designs for your special occasion.

www.oakscrossing-augusta.com

GUIDED BUS TOURS
The "Ladies Day Out" includes a guided tour of the shops in Defiance and Augusta, with a light breakfast at Frisella Nursery and lunch at Cafe Bella. Take a peek into the past with the "Historical Tour," where you'll visit St. Charles County historical sites in wine country and enjoy lunch at Wine Country Gardens. Finally, the "Taste of Missouri Wine" tour offers three different itineraries for visiting local wineries. All of the tours are offered on Wednesday through Friday and last from 9 a.m. to 5 p.m. Call Robin (of Robin's Nest) for additional information or to schedule a tour.

(314) 223-3423

HALCYON SPA & SALON

Rejuvenate and relax with a facial, bodywork, massage, or one of the many other soothing services. Extend the pampering with a day spa package, yoga at a local winery, waxing, or nail treatment. Cute gift items, yoga clothes, nutritious snacks, and other products can be purchased in the lounge area. Better yet, the inviting Halcyon Spa Bed & Breakfast is on-site, yet secluded, and includes a healthy breakfast delivered to your room, use of the sauna, a full spa bath with dual shower, a free yoga class when available, an outdoor seating area, a king-size bed, and a kitchenette. Find information about their services, weekend retreats, and pricing on the website.

(636) 228-4110
211 Jackson St., Augusta
www.halcyonaugusta.com

KATY BIKE RENTAL

To rent bikes and equipment, visit Katy Bike Rental at two locations. You can also get biking and other necessities, snacks (like Serendipity Ice Cream), and beverages here. Both stores can be accessed from the Katy Trail. Shuttle services are also available.

(636) 987-2673
2998 Hwy. 94 S,
Defiance
(626) 359-9095
5533 Water St., Augusta
www.katybikerental.com

MISSOURI RIVER EXCURSIONS

Missouri River Excursions rents canoes, kayaks, and large rafts for floaters. The outfitter will drop you off and pick you up from your route of choice. Guides are available for half-day or longer floats with several route options. Reservations are required and floaters must be at least 12 years old. Visit the website for additional pricing and information.

(636) 485-5163
2886 S Hwy. 94, Defiance
www.floatmissouririver.com

WELDON SPRING SITE

While at first it might seem an odd place to visit, the Weldon Spring site is full of interesting information, has countless interactive displays, and is an educational yet fun opportunity for families heading out to wine country. In the 1940s, the area was used by the U.S. Army to manufacture explosives. Concern for ground and water contamination upon the property led to testing, maintenance, and cleanup. The grounds have been deemed safe to visit, but are continuously monitored. Today, visitors can climb to the top of the 75-foot-high disposal cell for a panoramic view of St. Charles County and Howell Prairie, hike or bike the Hamburg Trail, visit the interpretive center, and observe wildflower spaces. For additional information, visit the website.

(636) 300-2600
7295 Hwy. 94, just a short distance from Hwy. 40, St. Charles
www.lm.doe.gov.weldon/Sites.aspx

kids

WINE WAGON SHUTTLE

This transportation service is available to individuals, for private parties, and during special events. Reservations are not required, but are highly recommended. The shuttle runs from 11 a.m. to 7 p.m. on Saturday and by reservation on Sunday during the spring, summer, and fall. Pick-up locations include the commuter lot located at Highways 40/94 and nearby hotels or bed & breakfasts. Make reservations by email or phone.

(314) 602-2696
winewagonshuttle@gmail.com
www.winewagonshuttle.com

FOR THE HISTORY BUFF

DANIEL BOONE HOME

In 1799, when Daniel Boone was 65 years old, the Spanish government offered him a land grant in what is now St. Charles County with the hope that his settling in the area would entice others to follow. Even during his lifetime, Boone was legendary for his explorations, leadership, and eye for good land. As Kentucky was growing too crowded for his tastes, Daniel Boone accepted the offer and moved his family to land that would one day be in Missouri.

The structure known as the Daniel Boone Home was actually the home of his youngest son, Nathan (Daniel's homesite was about four miles from the DBH). Daniel moved into a room on the first floor of the home in 1813, after his wife, Rebecca, died. He lived there until his death in 1820 at age 85. Nathan's land is also home to the "Judgment Tree," where Daniel often held court in his role as justice of the peace. The tree is not part of the Daniel Boone Home tour but is accessible from the Katy Trail.

The home is owned and operated today by Lindenwood University. It is open for tours and gives a snapshot of how a wealthy pioneer family might have lived in the early 1800s. The tours are a combination of historical lore and fact (clearly identified) led by entertaining and knowledgeable guides.

Since Lindenwood took over the Daniel Boone Home, a number of buildings dating to the early 1800s, including a church available for weddings, have been moved to the site, creating a facsimile of a pioneer village. Both guided and self-guided tours of the village are available.

The Heritage Center offers a variety of activities throughout the year: school visits, scout visits, interpreters who dress and act as characters from the time period, camps, and classes for both children and adults. Pioneer Days, scheduled annually in September, gives families a chance to engage in activities of the era. In October, the center hosts a Spirits from the Past Halloween Tour by lantern light, complete with spooky tales. December brings the annual Christmas Candlelight Tour with blazing candles and a taste of how Christmas was celebrated by pioneers in Missouri.

Open daily, 8:30 a.m.–5 p.m.
June 1 to September 30, 8:30 a.m.–6 p.m.
Special evening hours for events
Closed major holidays
(636) 798-2005
1868 Hwy. F, Defiance
boonehome@lindenwood.edu
www.danielboonehome.com

Admission for guided or self-guided tours of either the home or the village is $7 for adults, $6 for seniors, and $4 for children aged 4 to 11.

Admission for guided or self-guided tours of both the home and the village is $12 for adults, $10 for seniors, and $6 for children aged 4 to 11.

For wedding information, contact:
The Old Peace Chapel
(636) 398-5214
1868 Hwy. F, Defiance
peacechapel@lindenwood.edu

ST. CHARLES NEIGHBORHOODS – NORTHEAST

PORTAGE DES SIOUX

Portage des Sioux is a small community located in the southeast corner of St. Charles County where the Mississippi River and the Missouri River are only two miles apart. The name comes from the fact that Native Americans carried (portaged) their canoes across this neck of land to avoid a much longer trip by water.

A point of interest is the statue dedicated to "Our Lady of the Rivers." In 1951, a flood threatened to destroy the town, and citizens prayed to Mary, who for the first time was called Our Lady of the Rivers, to keep the town safe. The town was spared and a monument was built to thank and honor her.

The Blessing of the Fleet soon followed the erection of the Our Lady of the Rivers Shrine. Each year, decorated boats parade to the site of the statue to be blessed by the parish priest to keep them from harm.

A peace treaty between the United States and all warring Native American tribes in 1815 was signed at Portage des Sioux. A bicentennial celebration of the signing is planned for 2015.

OUR LADY OF THE RIVERS

COMMEMORATIVE AIR FORCE MISSOURI WING FLYING MUSEUM

Smartt Field served as a naval training station during World War II and still functions as an airport today. It is also the location of a hidden gem of a museum, the Commemorative Air Force, Missouri Wing, dedicated to preserving the memory of those who served during the war and the aircraft they flew. The museum, which had to be restored after the 1993 flood, houses an array of artifacts, uniforms, newspaper articles, items from the homefront, weapons, and equipment from World War II. There are displays of German and Japanese uniforms, weapons, and artifacts as well. Most important, however, is the collection of vintage aircraft that have been preserved and still fly. The collection includes a B-25 Mitchell, a TBM

Avenger, and an L-3E "Grasshopper." Thirty-minute flights are available at specified times (check the website) for $395. The guides are knowledgeable and eager to share information.

The museum is off the beaten path, but worth seeking out for anyone interested in aviation and/or World War II. Be sure to call ahead to check if the aircraft will be on-site because they frequently travel to air shows around the nation.

Admission is $2 for adults and $1 for children under 10.
Thursday and Saturday, 10 a.m.–2:30 p.m.
(636) 250-4515
St. Charles County Airport–Smartt Field
6390 Grafton Ferry Rd., Portage des Sioux
www.cafmo.org

kids

GOLDEN EAGLE FERRY
The Golden Eagle travels between the small town of Golden Eagle, Illinois, to St. Charles County, terminating on Golden Eagle Ferry Road. The ferry is in operation weather and conditions permitting.

(618) 535-5759
www.thecalhounferrycompany.com

GRAFTON FERRY
The Grafton Ferry carries vehicles and passengers between Grafton, Illinois, and St. Charles County, terminating near St. Charles County Airport. It is open May 1 to October 31, with service limited to weekends at times.

Open (peak times) Monday through Thursday, 6 a.m.–6 p.m.
Friday, 6 a.m.–9 p.m.
Saturday, 10 a.m.–10 p.m.
Sunday, 8 a.m.–8 p.m.
(800) 258-6645
www.thegraftonferry.com

WEST ALTON

Located on the western bank of the Mississippi River opposite Alton, Illinois, West Alton is situated at the confluence of the Missouri and Mississippi Rivers. The small town encompasses just over 37 square miles (a little more than eight of those are water) and is home to the Riverlands Migratory Bird Sanctuary, the Audubon Center, the Edward and Pat Jones–Confluence Point State Park, Missouri Department of Conservation areas, Dresser Island, and several US Army Corps of Engineers recreational areas.

The Riverlands Migratory Bird Sanctuary is on *St. Louis Magazine*'s A-List of things to do in the St. Louis region and draws visitors year-round. Birds within their natural habitat (marshes, prairies, and bottomland forests) can be watched from viewing platforms and bird blinds. Eight and a half miles of hiking trails can be experienced through self-guided or group tours. Tour topics include Eagle Watching, the Trumpeter Swan, the American White Pelican, and the Migration Tour and Talk. Lasting approximately one and a half hours, the tour begins with a 30-minute presentation (including a 12-minute movie), and then a naturalist/educator joins the group on their bus while narrating the drive through the Riverlands. A $100 group fee for 20 people or less applies, while larger groups require an additional $5 per person. To schedule a tour, contact Matthew Magoc at mmagoc@audubon.org or call (636) 899-0090. Directions to the Riverlands, full tour descriptions, and a map can be found at www.riverlands.audubon.org. Use the website to check for trail closings or to make an online donation.

The Audubon Center is located within the Riverlands at 301 Riverlands Way. Families, schools, and travelers looking for an enjoyable, yet educational experience visit the center. Water conservation and the Mississippi River are featured topics, while year-round temporary exhibits are on display. One annual exhibit includes vintage and contemporary decoys, duck stamps, artwork, and more. The wraparound deck is perfect for viewing and is handicap accessible. Picnic tables overlooking Ellis Bay, the Mini-Wetland Pond, and the Native Rain Garden with winding walkway are also popular features on the property. The center is open 8 a.m.–4 p.m. daily except on major holidays. Admission is FREE, but donations are greatly appreciated.

Within the Edward and Pat Jones–Confluence Point State Park, visitors can see Confluence Point, the location where the Mississippi and Missouri Rivers join. Lewis & Clark's Corps of Discovery set off on their exploration up the Missouri River from here, heading west. The park offers great opportunities to view bald eagles, raptors, and waterfowl, as well as other wildlife. The park is located at 1000 Riverlands Way.

The conservation and recreational areas, in addition to Dresser Island, are popular for hiking, fishing, hunting, and wildlife viewing. The City Park offers the use of pavilions, a ball diamond, a tractor pull track, and public restrooms, while visitors can spend a moment honoring veterans at the West Alton Memorial Park. There is also a children's park in town. It is recommended that travelers call ahead to check for road closures and contact departments directly for area rules and regulations.

HELPFUL WEBSITES

www.historicstcharles.com

www.greatriverroad.com

www.mdc.mo.gov

www.mvs.usace.army.mil

www.rendezvousinstcharles.com

www.preservationjournal.org

www.stcharlescitymo.gov

www.youranswerplace.org

www.stcharlesparks.com

www.mostateparks.com

www.streetscapemag.com

Keep in mind that many of the businesses and attractions listed have Facebook pages that are helpful for current hours or current specials going on. A helpful Facebook page for the St. Charles area in general is:

www.facebook.com/pages/365-things-to-do-in-st-charles-missouri

PHOTO CREDITS

Vicki Berger Erwin

Sara Boehlein

Vic & Ruth Ann Brown

Cities of Augusta, Dardenne Prairie City Hall Staff, Lake St. Louis, O'Fallon, St. Charles, St. Peters, and Wentzville

Designers Boutique & Gifts

Glenda Ell

Frisella Nursery

Greater St. Charles Convention & Visitors Bureau

Holly Haddox

Michael Henry

Kathy Kessler/Halcyon Spa

Michael Jacob Photography

Missouri State Parks

Darren Noelken

Randal Oaks

Paul Markworth

Painting with a Twist

Remington's

Lane Richter

Justine Riggs

Kara Roberson

Roemer Originals

Dale Rollings

Seven Stones Weingarten

Special Olympics of MO

Sam Stang

Stephen Thompson

Stone Soup Cottage

INDEX

370 Lakeside Park, 107, 113

9-11 Memorial: A Tribute to First Responders, 138

Adrenaline Zone, 93

Aholt Farms Seasons of Fun, 193

Aiello's Cigar Bar, 123

Alice's Tea Room, 20

All That Glitterz, 3

Allin's Diner, 72

Aly's Interiors, 118

Amerisports Bar & Grill, 38

Ameristar Casino Resort & Spa, 38

Ann's Bra Shop, 158

Antiques & Oak, 3

Apple Gate Inn B&B, 184

April's on Main, 3

Ara Spa, 39

Art and Painting Classes, 153

Atelier at Frenchtown, The, 57

Audubon Center, The, 202

Augusta, 175

Augusta Brewing Co., 176

Augusta Emporium, 189

Augusta Glass Studio, 189

Augusta Historical Museum, 193

Augusta Visitor Center, 193

Augusta Wine Country Inn, 184

Augusta Winery, 176

Augusta Wood Ltd., 189

Ava's Closet, 158

Backyard Resale & Antiques, 158

Bakery, The, 38

Balducci Vineyards, 176

Bar Louie, 72

Barnes & Noble, 98

Barton Brothers Antiques, 58

Baskin Robbins, 133

Bass Pro, 67

Baubles, Bites & Boots, 3

Bayard Street Antique Mall, 58

BC's Kitchen, 152

Bear Creek Golf Course, 164

Beau Monde Bridal/Wedding Gallery, 58

Bella Bride, 135

Bella Vino Wine Bar & Tapas, 20

Bemo's, 119

Bicentennial Park, 168

Big A's on the Riverfront, 20

Bike Stop Café, 20

Bittersweet Inn, 61

Black Sheep, The, 118

Blanchette, Louis, 1

Blanchette Park, 86

Blue Bird Yoga, 42

Blue Sky Cafe & Bar, 126

Bobby's Place, 21

Bombshell Bar & Grill, 21

Boone, Daniel, 197

Boone's Colonial Inn, 28

Boone's Lick Trail Cottage, 28

Boone's Lick Trail Inn, 28

Boschertown Grand Prix, 93

Bottleneck Blues Bar, 38
Boulevard Bride, 150
Boulevard Park, 155
Braddens Restaurant, 21
Bridge Fair Trade Market, 4
Bristol Seafood Grill, 126
Broemmelsiek Park, 168
Brunswick Zone XL, 108
Bugatti's Steak & Pasta, 38
C. Rallo Meat Company, 135
Cabin Fever Daze, 143
Café Angelina, 177
Caleco's, 101
Calisa Home Décor, 98
Candlelight Christmas Walk, 182
Candlelight Concert (First State Capitol), 30
Candlelight Tours (First State Capitol), 30
Canine Cookies N Cream Dog Bakery, 4
Capp's Restaurant, 127
Carnival Frozen Custard, 133
Casino Bar Deli, 38
Cassandra Erin Studio, 4
Cave Springs Lanes, 109
Celebrate St. Peters Community Festival, 112
Celebration of Lights, 143
Centennial Carriage Rides, 40
Centennial Farms, 194
Centuries Past Antiques, 4
Chandler Hill Vineyards, 177
Chill, 172
Christmas Candlelight Tour, 198
City Centre, 113
Civic Park, 145
Cobblestone Cottage, 4
Colonial Table, The, 21

Comic Book Relief, 67
Commemorative Air Force Missouri Wing Flying Museum, 200
Concetta's, 73
Conference Center at Oaks Crossing, 194
Conservatory, The, 40
Conservatory Guest Cottage, 185
Corner Bar, 73
Cornerstone Cafe, 73
Cottleville, 117
Cottleville Wine Seller, 119
Country House, 5
Country Inn and Suites, 29
Crazy Sushi, 101
Creativ Eats, 74
Crooked Tree Coffee House, 74
Crossing, The, 73
Daniel Boone Home, 197
Dardenne Prairie, 135
Dardenne Prairie City Hall Park, 145
Defiance, 175
Defiance Roadhouse, 177
Demolition Ball, 93
Design on a Dime, 69
Design2Brew, 138
Designer Like, 5
Designer Resale Boutique, 98
Designers Boutique & Gifts, 135
Deters Frozen Custard, 90
Di Olivas, 5
Dierbergs School of Cooking, 94
Different Stuff Collectibles, 69
Donatelli's Bistro, 152
Doozle's, 90
Dreamcatcher, 16
Drury Inn St. Peters, 106

Edward and Pat Jones–Confluence Point State Park, 203
Elements Herbal Apothecary, 5
Elmer's Tavern, 102
Embassy Suites St. Louis—St. Charles Hotel & Spa, 80
Enchanted Attic, The, 5
Enchantments, 5
English Shop, The, 5
Ethyl's Smokehouse & Saloon, 127
European Accent, 6
Exit 6 Brewery, 120
Fairfield Inn & Suites, 163
Falcon Diner, 38
Fall Fest & Street Dance, 143
Fall Harvest Festival, 183
Family Arena, The, 81
Fancy Feet Shoe Boutique, 6
Farmers Market, 45
Fast Lane Classic Cars, 81
Festival of the Little Hills (Fetes des Petite Côtes), 45
Fête de Glace, 46
Figuero's, 6
Finishing Touches by Charlotte, 6
Fireside Bar & Grill, 177
Fireside Treasures, 158
First Capitol Trading, 7
First Missouri State Capitol, 30
First Watch, 102
Flea Market, 159
Flower Petaler, The, 7
Food Truck Frenzy, 143
Fort Zumwalt Park, 147
Founders Park, 155
Foundry Art Centre, 36
Fountain Lakes Park, 86

Fox & Hound Antiques & Décor, 7
Framations Custom Framing and Art Gallery, 8
Fran's, 8
Frankie Tocco's Pizzeria, 21
French Connection Antiques, 58
Frenchtown Antique Mall & Collectibles, 59
Frenchtown Heritage Museum and Research Center, 59
Frenchtown, 57
Friperie, 8
Fritz's Frozen Custard, 115, 133, 172
Frontier Park, 46
"Fun Times" (publication), 167
Garden Café a la Fleur, 22
Garvey Décor, 69
Gazebo in Kister Park, 47
Gene's Shoes, 8
Georgetown Park, 146
Gift Nook, 8
Ginsey Rose, 9
Glass Workbench, 18
Glenmark Farms, 82
Golden Eagle Ferry, 201
Good Buy Girls, 69
Grafton Ferry, 201
Grand Hall (Foundry Art Centre), 36
Grand Opera House and Banquet Center, 41
Grandma's Cookies, 9
Grapevine Vacation Rentals, 185
Grapevine Wine Bistro & Visitor's Center, 178
Great Skate, 109
Greater St. Charles Convention and Visitors Bureau, 30, 47

Greatview Bed & Breakfast, 185
Guided Bus Tours, 194
H.A.M.'s Deli, 22
H.S. Clay House, 186
Halcyon Spa & Salon, 195
Hampton Inn, 80
Hardware of the Past, 9
Haviland Museum, 32
Hawk Ridge Park, 156
Heald Home, 147
Heald, Nathan, 147
Heald, Rebekah, 147
Heatherbrook Park, 89
Hendricks BBQ, 22
Henry, Dr. Michael, 43
Heritage & Freedom Fest, 143
Heritage Center, 198
Hide & Chic by Double K Leather, 9
Hilton Garden Inn, 137
Historic Main Street, 1
Hobbit's Hole Antiques, 9
Hobos, 103
Hoeft Vineyard, 183
Holiday House, 7
Holy Grail Winery, 178
Homestead, The, 10
I-70 Shoppers Fair, 69
Indian Camp Creek Park, 168
Inn at Defiance, 186
Inspired, 70
J. Noto Bakery Fine Italian Confections, 10
Jake's on Main, 10
Jean Baptiste Point Dusable Park, 87
Jefferson Guest House B&B, 187
Jim & Deb's Lakeside Pub, 152

JJ Twig's Pizza & Pub, 128
Jo-Jo'z Frozen Yogurt, 133
Joe's Crab Shack, 103
Johann's General Store, 190
John Dengler, Tobacconist, 10
Joys by Austin Warren Design, 11
Jump 4 Fun, 138
Kate's Coffee House, 178
Katy Bike Rental, 195
Katy Trail State Park, 48
Kernel Dave's Gourmet Popcorn, 11
Kimberly's Bake Shop, 160
King Cat Club, 38
KiTARO Bistro of Japan, 128
Klondike Park, 187, 191
Kokomo Joe's Family Fun Center, 109
Kristkindlmarkt, 45
L'Auberge St. Charles Guest House, 61
La Carreta, 75
La Gallerie, 11
La Roserie, 11
Lady Bugs, 11
Lady Di's Diner, 75
Lake St. Louis, 149
Lake St. Louis Farmers and Artists Market, 150
Lake St. Louis Triathlon, 153
Laura's La Petite, 11
Laurel Park, 114
Legacy Park, 124
Lewis and Clark Boat House and Nature Center, 33
Lewis & Clark Fife and Drum Corps, 48
Lewis and Clark Heritage Days, 49
Lewis & Clark's Restaurant, 22
Lil' Shoppe of Treasures, 60
Lillian Yahn Gallery, 139

Lillian's, 11
Lindenwood Ice Arena, 164
Lindenwood University, 65, 82, 198
Little Hills Cottage, 12
Little Hills Wine Shop, 12
Little Hills Winery and Restaurant, 22
Little O's Old Time Soda Fountain, 23
Liz's Bar & Grill, 179
Lloyd & Harry's Bar & Grill, 23
Llywelyn's Pub, 23
Lococo House II and III, 61
Log Cabin Museum, 139
Los Portales Mexican Restaurant & Grocery, 160
Lulu's Shaved Ice, 173
Lyons Frozen Custard, 91
Maggie Malones, 160
Magpie Café, 23
Main Street Books, 12
Main Street Diner, 104
Main Street Guest House, 29
Main Street Gym, 42
Main Street Marketplace, 12
Main Street Root Beer and Soda, 12
Mannino's Market, 118
Marie Angelique Bra and Lingerie, 12
Mario's Donuts & Cafe, 104
Massa's, 76, 129
Master's Pieces Fine Jewelry & Gifts, 13
Matson Hill Park, 191
McGurk's Public House, 129
McNair Park, 87
Meadows, The, 151
Memories in the Attic, 13
Mid Rivers 14 Cine, 110
Mid Rivers Mall, 98

Miss Aimee B's Tea Room and Gallery, 76
Miss Ellie's Garden Inn, 187
Missouri Artists on Main, 13
Missouri Department of Conservation, The, 192
Missouri Mercantile, 13
Missouri River Excursions, 196
Missouri River Irish Fest, 50
Missouri Tartan Day Festivities, 50
Mom's Family Resale, 136
Montelle Winery, 179
MOSAICS Missouri Festival for the Arts, 51
Moss Boutique, 14
Mother-in-Law House Restaurant, 24
Mount Pleasant Estates, 179
Move It On & More, 70
Music on Main, 51
My Handyworks, 14
My Son's Cake & Candy Supply, 99
National Equestrian Center, 153
Native Traditions Gallery, 14
New Melle, 175
Nic Nac Stop, 14
Noboleis Vineyards, 180
O'Fallon, 125, 135
O'Fallon Founders' Day, 144
O'Fallon Jammin', 144
O'Fallon Main Street Marketplace, 136
Oberweis Dairy, 115
October Harvest, 112
Oktoberfest, 51
Old Borromeo Church, 34
Old Millstream Inn, 24
Old Stone Chapel and Banquet Center, 41

Old Town Guest House, 29
Old Towne Park, 114
Olde Town Spice Shoppe, 15
Omar J. Dames War Memorial, 139
Ooh La La, 15
Ooh La La Children's Boutique, 15
Orange Leaf Frozen Yogurt, 116, 134
Our Lady of the Rivers Shrine, 199
Ozzie Smith Sports Complex, 140
Painted Pot, The, 94
Painting with a Twist, 141
Pantera's Pizza, 130
Parkview Gardens, 83
Pearl's Oyster Bar, 38
Piazza Deli & Pizzeria, 180
Picasso's Coffee House, 25
Piggy's Bar BQ, 130
Pioneer Days, 198
Pio's Restaurant and Cocktail Lounge, 76
Pirrone's Pizza, 105
Plank Road Pizza, 120
Playtime Party Center, 165
Plein Air Art Festival, 183
Polar Plunge, 154
Poor Man's Art Gallery, 15
Pop A Wheelie on the Katy Trail, 180
Poppy's Amish Cupboard, 15
Portage des Sioux, 199
Prasino, 77
Provenance Soapworks, 15
Pump It Up, 95
Quail Ridge Park, 169
Quilted Cottage, The, 15
Quintessential Dining & Nightlife, 25
R. T. Weiler's Food and Spirits, 25
Rack House West Winery, 121

Red Door Furniture Company, 57
Red Posie Vintage Resale, 70
Regal O'Fallon Stadium 14, 141
Remington's, 16
Renaud Spirit Center, 141
Rendezvous Cafe & Wine Bar, 130
Residence Inn, 137
Riverfest, 52
Riverfront Guest House, 29
Riverlands Migratory Bird Sanctuary, 202
Riverside Sweets, 16
Robin's Nest on the Katy Trail, 190
Roemer Originals, 67
Rotary Park, 169
St. Charles, 65
St. Charles Antique Mall, 71
St. Charles City-County Library District, 83
St. Charles Convention Center, 84
St. Charles County Amateur Sports Hall of Fame, 140
St. Charles County Community College, 110
St. Charles County Historical Society, 35
St. Charles Ghost Tours, 43
St. Charles Heritage Museum and Park, 88
St. Charles Municipal Band Concerts, 52
St. Louis Renaissance Faire, 166
St. Pat's Day Parade and Run for the Helmet, 123
St. Peters, 97
St. Peters Cultural Arts Centre, 110
St. Peters Golf & Recreation Center, 114
St. Peters Rec-Plex, 111
Scentchips St. Charles, 16

Schnarr Jewelers, 16
Se7en Cupcakes and Martinis, 121
Secondhand Chic Marketplace, 60
Señora Espinos Taqueria, 131
Seven Stones Weingarten, 180
Shabby Road, A, 57
Shamrocks Pub n Grill, 105
Shoppes at Hawk Ridge Shopping Center, 151
Shrine of St. Rose Philippine Duchesne, 63
Silky's Frozen Custard, 116
Siostra, 16
Skateboard Park, 95
Smoothie King, 91, 134, 173
Snibo's Sports Bar, 105
Spirits from the Past Halloween Tour, 198
Spiro's Restaurant, 77
Splash Station Aquatic Center, 170
Steel Shop Tennis Club, 42
Stefanina's Italian Restaurant, 161
Stefanina's Pizzeria & Restaurant, 132
Steve's Produce, 68
Stitches, Etc, 17
Stone Ledge Antiques, 190
Stone Ledge Guest Suite B&B, 188
Stone Soup Cottage, 122
String Along With Me, 17
Studio Gallo Blu, 17
Sugar Creek Winery, 181
Sugarfire Smoke House, 78, 132
Sundermeier RV Park, 62
Sunny Street Cafe, 161
Sunset Fridays, 112
Susie Q Quilting, 136
Swing-A-Round, 96
Swingin' in the Vines, 183

T. R. Hughes Ballpark, 140
Talayna's World Class Pizza, 26
Tap Restaurant & Brewery, 78
Tattooed Dog, 161
Texas Smokehouse Saloon, 161
Thistle and Clover, 17
Thro's Clothing Company and Michelle's, 17
Through the Looking Glass, 20
Tic-Top Shop, 136
Tiffany Garden, 18
Tintypery, The, 18
Tony's on Main Street, 26
Tony's on Top, 26
Toodaloo, 19
Towne Park, 171
Trading Post, The (Lewis and Clark Boat House), 34
Trailhead Brewing Company, 27
Treats Unleashed, 99
Tree Lighting Ceremony, 144
Tren-Deez Village, 71
Trick or Treat on Main Street, 53
Tubby's Pub 'n Grub, 79
Tucanos Brazilian Grill, 79
Tuner's Restaurant and Bar, 27
U-Swirl Frozen Yogurt, 92
Uncle Joe's Bar and Grill, 27
Undertow, 27
Unkorked Wine Garden, 162
USA Resale, 159
Vaccaro & Sons Produce, 68
Valenti's Market & Catering Co., 99
Vantage Park, 124
Veterans Memorial Park, 156
Veterans Memorial Walk, 142
Wabash Days Festival, 166

Wacky Warriors Paintball, 165

Walk of Discovery (Lewis and Clark Boat House), 34

Walter's Jewelry, 19

Wapelhorst Park, 89

Webster Park, 89

Wehrenberg St. Charles Stadium 18 Cine, 85

Wehrenberg Town Square 12 Cine, 142

Weldon Spring Site, 196

Wentzville, 157

Wentzville Donut Cafe, 162

West Allen Grill, 162

West Alton, 202

Westoff Park, 146

White Hare, The, 100

White Traditions Bridal House, 60

Wine Country Gardens, 181

Wine Wagon Shuttle, 196

Wise Owl Resale, 71

Wooden Door, The, 159

Worn Vintage, 60

Yellow Farmhouse Winery, 181

Yo My Goodness, 92

Youth Activity Park, 146

Zumwalt, Jacob, 147